ITALY AND ITS CUISINE

Recipes Selected and Edited by Jillian Stewart
Designed by Alison Jewell
Jacket Design by Justine Davies
Food Photography by Peter Barry and
Neil Sutherland

MALLARD PRESS

An imprint of BDD Promotional Book Company, Inc.,
666 Fifth Avenue, New York, N.Y. 10103.
Mallard Press and its accompanying design and logo
are trademarks of BDD Promotional Book Company, Inc.

CLB 2371
Copyright © 1991 Colour Library Books Ltd.,
Godalming, Surrey, England.
Text filmsetting by Words and Spaces, Hampshire England.
First published in the United States of America
in 1991 by the Mallard Press.
Printed and bound in Hong Kong.
All rights reserved
ISBN 0 792 45228 3

ITALY
AND ITS
CUISINE

MALLARD
PRESS

CONTENTS

*Title page: Home-made Tagliatelle with
Summer Sauce.*

*Previous pages: the Ponte Vecchio, Florence,
and (inset) Tomato Salad Rustica. These pages:
Lago di Carezza, in the Dolomites. Overleaf: a
gondolier in traditional dress plies the waters of
Venice.*

INTRODUCTION

Italian cuisine has long been a great favorite throughout the world, its simplicity, style and variety endearing it to an ever-growing number of devotees.

One of the biggest attractions of Italian cooking is its regional diversity. Almost every corner of Italy has nurtured and developed its own distinctive specialties and style of cookery. Italy only came together as a united country in 1861 and it is therefore understandable that these regional variations are still very much in evidence. Tuscany is famous for its delicious veal, cooked in a simple, yet elegant manner, while Neapolitan cooking is characterized by the use of tomatoes and garlic. Naples, on the other hand, is credited with that most popular of Italian exports, the pizza, whilst the rich waters of the Adriatic and Tyrrhenian seas provide the fish and seafood so popular with the tourists in the street cafés of Veneto.

Throughout its history many influences have shaped the course of Italian cuisine. The early Romans were notorious for the huge, lavish banquets that they bestowed upon guests. They were also successful farmers who utilized methods developed by the Greeks to cultivate vegetables and rear livestock. Early cooking methods were extremely rudimentary and not until the Renaissance did cooks begin to experiment with subtle ways of enhancing the taste of a meal rather than masking its flavor with overpowering sauces and spices.

The Renaissance saw a move away from traditional carnivorous feasts to lighter treats such as pasta and the delicious truffles of the Piedmont region. The process of eating also became a far more refined affair, with Italy's richest families taking pride in their lavish dinnerware and cutlery. Indeed, the Italian court was at this point so innovative that in 1533 when Catherine De Medici married the future king of France, she insisted on taking her personal cooks to the French court. At this time French cooking lacked the imagination and style shown by the Italian chefs, who later proved to have a great influence on the blossoming of French cuisine.

In contrast to the extravagant and rich foods eaten by the wealthy, the food of the ordinary citizen was very much dependent on simple local produce. Today, Italian cooking follows this tradition and relies on varied and imaginative use of fresh, good quality ingredients, especially vegetables and herbs. Many Italians still follow the old tradition of growing herbs and fresh vegetables for their own use, and the exuberant exchanges in any Italian market testify to the importance of fresh, top quality produce for those who do not grow their own.

One of the features of Italian mealtimes is that they are lively and lengthy social events. The whole family gathers round to gossip and, most of all, to enjoy the food. When serving an Italian meal bear in mind the exuberance which is part of the Italian temperament whether they are doing the cooking, eating or serving! There are very few Italian restaurants where the atmosphere is subdued and conversation quiet. This is because food in Italy is part of life – to be enjoyed and savored whether it is being served at home or in the local trattoria!

Along with a genuine Italian atmosphere goes the actual authenticity of the meal. Don't be tempted to serve only one dish – Italian family meals consist of a whole range of different dishes such as risotto, polenta, fresh vegetables, salads, sausages, roast meats, cheeses, pasta and fresh fruit, and of course, wine.

So whether you are planning a family meal or an impressive dinner party, an authentic taste of Italy is at your fingertips with the deliciously creative recipes which make up *Italy and its Cuisine*.

SERVES 4

Fish Soup

An unusual soup which is sure to be admired by the most critical dinner guest.

PREPARATION TIME: 15 minutes
COOKING TIME: 40 minutes

2lbs of bass, whiting, monkfish and/or bream, skin and bones removed, and cut into bite-size pieces
2 onions, peeled and chopped
3 cloves garlic, minced
2 tomatoes, skinned and chopped
1 tbsp oil
Sprig of fresh thyme

1 bay leaf
2 pieces thinly pared orange rind
½ cup dry white wine
Salt
Pepper

GARNISH
Chopped parsley

Make a broth with the heads and trimmings of fish, one-third of the onion and 5 cups of water. Simmer for 15 minutes, then strain. Put oil in a heavy pan and heat gently. Add garlic and remaining onion. Cover and fry gently for 5 minutes without coloring. Add fish, tomatoes, herbs, orange rind, wine, salt and pepper and broth. Bring to boil and simmer for 10 minutes. Remove bay leaf, thyme and orange rind. Serve hot, sprinkled with parsley.

SERVES 4

Lobster Cream Soup

This mouthwatering soup is the perfect choice when you want to impress your guests.

PREPARATION TIME: 20 minutes
COOKING TIME: 1 hour

1 cooked lobster
1 onion, peeled and diced
1 stick celery, cut into 1-inch slices
1 carrot, diced
5 cups fish stock or water
1 bay leaf
6 peppercorns
Parsley stalks
Salt
Pepper

2 tbsps butter or margarine
2 tbsps flour
1 tsp lemon juice
2 tbsps cream
3 tbsps white wine
2 tsps tomato paste

GARNISH
Cream and chopped parsley

Remove meat from body, tail and claws of lobster. Put lobster shell, stock or water, onion, carrot, celery, herbs and seasoning into a pan. Bring to boil and simmer for 45 minutes. Allow to cool. Strain and reserve stock. Meanwhile, cut lobster meat into bite-size pieces. Melt butter in pan, stir in flour, and cook for 1 minute. Remove from heat and stir in reserved stock gradually. Return to heat. Bring to the boil, and simmer for 5 minutes, stirring continuously. Remove from heat and add lemon juice, tomato paste, wine and cream, and whisk in well. Adjust seasoning. Add lobster meat and garnish with cream and chopped parsley if desired. Serve immediately.

SERVES 4-6

Spinach Gnocchi

Gnocchi are dumplings that are served like pasta. A dish of gnocchi can be served as a first course or as a light main course, sprinkled with cheese or accompanied by a sauce.

PREPARATION TIME: 15 minutes
COOKING TIME: 20 minutes

4oz chopped, frozen spinach
8oz ricotta cheese
3oz Parmesan cheese
Salt and pepper

Freshly shredded nutmeg
1 egg, slightly beaten
3 tbsps butter

Defrost the spinach and press it between two plates to extract all the moisture. Mix the spinach with the ricotta cheese, half the Parmesan cheese, salt, pepper and nutmeg. Gradually add the egg, beating well until the mixture holds together when shaped. With floured hands, form the mixture into oval shapes. Use about 1 tbsp mixture for each gnocchi. Lower into simmering water, 3 or 4 at a time, and allow to cook gently until the gnocchi float to the surface, about 1-2 minutes. Remove with a draining spoon and place in a well-buttered ovenproof dish. When all the gnocchi are cooked, sprinkle on the remaining Parmesan cheese and dot with the remaining butter. Reheat for 10 minutes in a hot oven and brown under a preheated broiler before serving.

Above: the town of Ancona, on the Adriatic coast has become one of the most important industrial towns in the Marche region.

SERVES 4

Shrimp in Melons

A simple yet creative dish which will leave the cook unruffled and the guests delighted.

PREPARATION TIME: 25 minutes

2 small melons
8oz peeled shrimp
Juice of half a lemon
1 small cucumber
4 medium-sized tomatoes
⅓ cup toasted flaked almonds
1 orange

4 tbsps light vegetable oil
Salt
Pepper
2 tbsps chopped basil
Pinch of sugar
1 tsp chopped lemon thyme
(optional)

Cut melons in half through the middle and scoop out flesh with a melon-baller or spoon, leaving a ¼-inch border of fruit on the inside of each shell. Cut a thin slice off the bottom of each shell so that they stand upright. Peel cucumber, cut in half lengthwise, then into ½-inch cubes. Peel and squeeze seeds from tomatoes and cut tomatoes into strips. Peel and segment orange. Mix lemon juice and oil together for the dressing. Add chopped basil and thyme (if desired), a pinch of sugar, and salt and pepper to taste. Toss fruit and vegetables together with the shrimp. Pile ingredients evenly into each melon shell. Chill well and garnish with the almonds.

Right: local fishing boats shelter along the rugged coastline and high cliffs of Amalfi, on the Sorrento peninsula.

Hot Vegetable Dip

Serve this delicious dip with a variety of vegetables such as celery, cabbage, cauliflower and green peppers.

PREPARATION TIME: 5 minutes
COOKING TIME: 5-10 minutes

3 cloves garlic
1 cup olive oil

¼ cup anchovies in oil, chopped

Cut garlic cloves into very thin strips and sauté them in oil until soft. Keep garlic from browning and consequently losing its flavor. Remove pan from heat and add anchovies. Crush anchovies with wooden spoon. Replace on heat and keep hot.

Venice's unique canals crisscross a city constantly under threat from rising water levels.

SERVES 4

Fanned Avocado Salad with Shrimp and Tomato Dressing

This colorful and impressive appetizer is simple to prepare and tastes delicious.

PREPARATION TIME: 20 minutes

2 ripe avocados
Juice of ½ lemon or 1 lime
8oz shrimp, shelled and deveined
3 tbsps mayonnaise
1 tbsp tomato paste
1 tbsp light cream

Salt
Pepper
GARNISH
Lemon or lime rings
Lettuce leaves

Mix together the mayonnaise, tomato paste, cream and salt and pepper to taste. Mix shrimp with 2 tbsps mayonnaise mixture and set aside. Cut avocados in half. Remove stones and peel back and remove skin. Slice down through flesh 5 or 6 times. Keep thin end intact. Place on lettuce leaves on serving dishes and press down so that the avocado fans out. Sprinkle over lemon or lime juice to prevent flesh browning. Place shrimp at side of dish, around avocado. Garnish with lemon or lime rings.

Above: one of the Swiss guards who act as bodyguards to the pope in the Vatican City.

SERVES 4-6

Bean Soup

Beans are a great favorite in Italy. In this recipe kidney beans are mixed with bacon and celery to produce a tasty and filling soup.

PREPARATION TIME: 15 minutes
COOKING TIME: 1 hour 45 minutes

15oz can kidney beans
2 strips bacon, chopped
1 stick celery, chopped
1 small onion, peeled and chopped
1 clove garlic, minced
½ cup plum tomatoes, chopped and seeds removed

4 cups water
1 chicken bouillon cube
1 tbsp chopped parsley
1 tsp basil
1 cup whole-wheat ring pasta
Salt and pepper

Place kidney beans, bacon, celery, onion, garlic, parsley, basil, tomatoes and water in a large pan. Bring to the boil and add bouillon cube and salt and pepper to taste. Cover and cook over a low heat for about 1½ hours. Raise heat and add pasta, stirring well. Stir frequently until the pasta is cooked but still firm, about 10 minutes. Serve immediately.

SERVES 4-6

Tomato Soup

Macaroni and green pepper add extra interest to this delicious soup.

PREPARATION TIME: 15 minutes
COOKING TIME: 45 minutes

1 cup short-cut/elbow macaroni
2 tbsps butter or margarine
1 small onion, peeled and chopped
1 small green pepper, cored, seeded, and chopped
1 tbsp flour
1 quart brown stock, or water plus
2 beef bouillon cubes

1lb tomatoes, chopped
2 tbsps tomato paste
1 tbsp grated horseradish
Salt and pepper

GARNISH
2 tbsps soured cream
1 tbsp chopped parsley

Heat the butter in a pan. Add the onion and green pepper, cover and cook for 5 minutes. Add the flour and stir. Add stock, tomatoes and tomato paste. Simmer for 15 minutes. Purée the soup and strain. Return soup to the pan, and season with salt and pepper to taste. Add macaroni 10 minutes before serving. Simmer and stir occasionally. Add horseradish before serving. Garnish with soured cream and parsley. Serve immediately.

Above: many of Italy's northern areas reflect the close proximity of Switzerland.

SERVES 4

Scallops au Gratin

This recipe makes the most of the delicious scallops found off Italy's beautiful coast.

PREPARATION TIME: 10 minutes

COOKING TIME: 15 minutes

4 scallops
2-3 tbsps finely chopped shallots (a small onion will do)
2 tbsps oil
¼ cup butter

1 wineglass of white wine
2 egg yolks
¼ cup shredded fontina cheese
4 tbsps white breadcrumbs
2 tbsps heavy cream

Heat the oil and butter in a heavy frying pan. Add the shallots and cook gently until they soften. Slice the white parts of the scallops. Increase the heat, stir in the white wine and then the sliced scallops and cook fairly briskly for 2-3 minutes. Slice the coral of the scallops and add to the pan, cooking the mixture for a further minute. Add the cream to the lightly beaten egg yolks. Stir gently over a low heat until the mixture thickens, adding a sprinkling of salt and pepper. Divide between four scallop shells, making sure each one has its fair share of the coral. Place 1 tbsp of cheese and 1 tbsp of breadcrumbs on each and place under the heated broiler until just beginning to brown on top. Serve immediately with brown bread.

Stuffed Tomatoes

Serve these colorful tomatoes as an appetizer or as a light lunch or supper dish.

PREPARATION TIME: 10 minutes
COOKING TIME: 20 minutes

4 large ripe tomtoes
1lb fresh spinach
¼ tsp shredded nutmeg
2 tbsps butter, creamed
¾ cup soup pasta
1 tbsp heavy cream

1 clove garlic, minced
1 tbsp Gruyère or Cheddar cheese, shredded
4 anchovies, sliced
Salt and pepper

Cut tops off tomatoes and carefully scoop out the insides with a teaspoon. Wash spinach well and remove stalks. Cook gently in a large saucepan, without added water, until spinach is soft. Chop spinach very finely, or blend in a food processor. Meanwhile, cook pasta for 5 minutes, or until tender. Rinse and drain well. Mix with the spinach. Add butter, cream, nutmeg and garlic, and season well. Fill each tomato and top with cheese and anchovies. Bake in oven at 350°F, for 10 minutes. Serve immediately.

The small Tuscan town of Peralta sleeps in the heat of the afternoon sun.

SERVES 4

Onion-Egg-Tomato Bake

A cheap and cheerful dish which is sure to please both children and adults.

PREPARATION TIME: 15 minutes

COOKING TIME: 20 minutes

4 eggs, hard-cooked	1 tbsp breadcrumbs
2 medium-sized onions, peeled and	1 tbsp freshly shredded Parmesan
sliced	cheese
4 tbsps butter or margarine	Salt
2 tbsps flour	Pepper
⅔ cup milk	
2 tomatoes, skinned and	**GARNISH**
sliced thinly	Parsley

Melt the butter in a pan. Add onions and fry over gentle heat until softened but not colored. Remove with a slotted spoon and set aside. Stir in flour and cook for 1 minute. Remove from heat and gradually stir in milk. Beat well and return to heat. Cook for 3 minutes, stirring continuously. Add onions and plenty of salt and pepper to counteract the sweetness of the onions. Cut eggs in half. Remove yolks, strain and set aside. Rinse and slice egg whites. Place in the bottom of an ovenproof dish. Cover with onion mixture, then with a layer of sliced tomatoes. Mix together egg yolk, breadcrumbs and Parmesan cheese. Sprinkle over top and place in oven at 400°F until golden on top. Garnish with parsley.

SERVES 4

Broccoli Timbales

This light appetizer is the perfect start to an extensive dinner party menu.

PREPARATION TIME: 10 minutes

COOKING TIME: 30 minutes

4 broccoli flowerets	1 tsp ground nutmeg
2 tbsps butter or margarine	2 eggs, beaten
2 tbsps flour	Salt
1¼ cups milk	Pepper

Blanch broccoli in boiled salted water for 3 minutes. Drain and refresh under cold water. Drain and set aside. Melt butter in pan. Stir in flour and nutmeg and cook for 1 minute. Remove from heat and stir in milk gradually. Return to heat and bring to the boil, stirring continuously. Cook for 3 minutes. Add salt and white pepper to taste and beat well. Set aside to cool. Butter 4 custard cups. Place a floweret of broccoli in each cup with stem pointing upwards. Beat eggs into cooled white sauce, and pour into each custard cup. Place cups in a shallow baking pan. Pour boiling water into pan to a depth of 1-inch. Bake in a preheated oven at 375°F for 15 minutes, or until just setting. Remove from oven and turn out onto individual plates. Serve immediately.

SERVES 4

Pepper Appetizer

This colorful appetizer is full of the flavor and simplicity of authentic Italian cuisine.

PREPARATION TIME: 15 minutes
COOKING TIME: 1 hour 15 minutes

1 green pepper	Salt
1 red pepper	2 tbsps oil
2 tomatoes	¼ cup white vinegar
2 onions	

Remove core and seeds from peppers and slice lengthwise. Peel and slice tomatoes and onions. Heat oil in a large saucepan. Add vegetables, salt to taste, and simmer, covered, for 1 hour, stirring occasionally. Remove lid and add vinegar, and simmer for a further 15 minutes. Allow to cool, and chill in refrigerator before serving.

Left: la Marina Piccola on the picturesque island of Capri.

SERVES 4

Fish Ravioli

Serve this marvellous dish at a family gathering, where it is sure to please every generation.

PREPARATION TIME: 30 minutes

COOKING TIME: 30 minutes

DOUGH
1¼ cups bread flour
Pinch of salt
3 eggs

FILLING
½lb sole fillets, or flounder, skinned and boned
2 tbsps breadcrumbs
2 eggs, beaten
1 green onion, finely chopped
1 slice of onion
1 slice of lemon
6 peppercorns

1 bay leaf
1 tbsp lemon juice
1 cup water

LEMON SAUCE
2 tbsps butter or margarine
2 tbsps flour
1 cup strained cooking liquid from fish
2 tbsps heavy cream
2 tbsps lemon juice
Salt
Pepper

To make filling
Preheat oven. Wash and dry fish. Place in ovenproof dish with onion, slice of lemon, peppercorns, bay leaf, lemon juice and water. Cover and cook in oven at 350°F for 20 minutes. Remove fish from liquid, and allow to drain. Strain liquid and set aside. When fish is cool, beat with the back of a spoon to a pulp. Add eggs, breadcrumbs and green onion, and salt and pepper to taste. Mix well.

To make dough
Sift flour into a bowl. Make a well in the center and add the eggs. Work the flour and eggs together with a spoon, and then knead by hand, until a smooth dough is formed. Leave to rest for 15 minutes. Lightly flour a board, and roll out dough thinly into a rectangle. Cut dough in half. Shape the filling into small balls, and set them about 1½-inches apart on one half of the dough. Place the other half on top, and cut with a ravioli cutter or small pastry cutter. Seal the edges. Cook in batches in a large, wide pan with plenty of boiling salted water until tender – about 8 minutes. Remove carefully with a perforated spoon. Meanwhile, make sauce.

To make sauce
Melt butter in pan. Stir in flour, and cook for 30 seconds. Draw off heat, and gradually stir in liquid from cooked fish. Return to heat and bring to boil. Simmer for 4 minutes, stirring continuously. Add cream and mix well. Season to taste. Remove from heat, and gradually stir in lemon juice. Do not reboil. Pour sauce over ravioli and serve immediately.

SERVES 6-8

Seafood Torta

A very stylish version of a fish flan, this makes a perfect accompaniment
to an Italian aperitif, or serves as a light supper dish with salad.

PREPARATION TIME: 35 minutes
plus 1 hour refrigeration
COOKING TIME: 40 minutes

DOUGH
2 cups all-purpose flour, sifted
½ cup unsalted butter
Pinch salt
4 tbsps cold milk

FILLING
4oz whitefish fillets (plaice, sole or
cod)
8oz cooked shrimp
4oz flaked crab meat

½ cup white wine
½ cup water
Large pinch hot pepper flakes
Salt and pepper
2 tbsps butter
2 tbsps flour
1 clove garlic, minced
2 egg yolks
½ cup heavy cream
Chopped fresh parsley

To prepare the dough, sift the flour into a bowl or onto a work surface. Cut the butter
into small pieces and begin mixing them into the flour. Mix until the mixture
resembles fine breadcrumbs – this may also be done in a food processor. Make a well in
the flour, pour in the milk and add the pinch of salt. Mix with a fork, gradually
incorporating the butter and flour mixture from the sides until all the ingredients are
mixed. This may also be done in a food processor. Form the dough into a ball and
knead for about 1 minute. Leave the dough in the refrigerator for about 1 hour.

To prepare the filling, cook whitefish fillets in the water and wine with the red
pepper flakes for about 10 minutes or until just firm to the touch. When the fish is
cooked, remove it from the liquid and flake it into a bowl with the shrimp and the crab
meat. Reserve the cooking liquid.

Melt the butter in a small saucepan and stir in the flour. Gradually strain on the
cooking liquid from the fish, stirring constantly until smooth. Add garlic, place over
high heat and bring to the boil. Lower the heat and allow to cook for 1 minute. Add to
the fish in the bowl and set aside to cool.

On a well-floured surface, roll out the dough and transfer it with a rolling pin to a
tart pan with a removable base. Press the dough into the pan and cut off any excess.
Prick the dough base lightly with a fork and place a sheet of wax paper inside. Fill with
rice, dried beans or baking beans and chill for 30 minutes. Bake the pastry shell blind
for 15 minutes in a 375°F oven. While the dough is baking, combine the egg yolks,
cream and parsley and stir into the fish filling. Adjust the seasoning with salt and
pepper. When the dough is ready, remove the paper and beans and pour in the filling.
Return the tart to the oven and bake for a further 25 minutes. Allow to cool slightly
and then remove from the pan. Transfer to a serving dish and slice before serving.

SERVES 4
Crab Cannelloni

Crab is always special, combined with cannelloni it is absolutely delicious.

PREPARATION TIME: 10 minutes
COOKING TIME: 40 minutes

12 cannelloni shells

FILLING
½lb fresh crab meat (or frozen crab
    meat, thawed)
2 tbsps butter or margarine
3 shallots, peeled and chopped
½ tsp Worcestershire sauce
1 tsp Dijon mustard
Salt
Pepper

MORNAY SAUCE
2 tbsps butter or margarine
2 tbsps flour
1¼ cups milk
¼ cup Cheddar or Parmesan
    cheese, shredded
Salt
Pepper

Cook cannelloni shells in a large pan of boiling salted water for 15-20 minutes until tender. Rinse in hot water and drain well. Meanwhile, heat butter in pan. Add shallots, crab meat, Worcestershire sauce, mustard, salt and pepper, and stir until heated through. Fill cannelloni shells with crab mixture, using a pastry bag with a wide, plain nozzle, or a teaspoon. Place in an ovenproof dish.

To make mornay sauce
Heat butter in pan and stir in flour. Remove from heat and gradually add milk. Return to heat and bring to boil. Cook for 3 minutes, stirring continuously. Stir in half the cheese until it melts. Do not reboil. Season with salt and pepper. Pour over the cannelloni and sprinkle with remaining cheese. Place in oven at 400°F, or under a broiler until golden brown. Serve immediately.

The elaborately decorated gondolas of Venice are the perfect vehicle for exploring the city in comfort and style.

SERVES 4-6

Swordfish Kebabs

Swordfish is one of the most commonly caught fish in Southern Italy and Sicily. It won't fall apart during cooking – a bonus when making kebabs.

PREPARATION TIME: 15 minutes
COOKING TIME: 10 minutes

2¼lbs swordfish steaks
6 tbsps olive oil
1 tsp chopped oregano
1 tsp chopped marjoram
Juice and rind of ½ a lemon

4 tomatoes, cut in thick slices
2 lemons, cut in thin slices
Salt and freshly ground pepper
Lemon slices and Italian parsley
for garnish

Cut the swordfish steaks in 2-inch pieces. Mix the olive oil, herbs, lemon juice and rind together and set it aside. Thread the swordfish, tomato slices and lemon slices on skewers, alternating the ingredients. Brush the skewers with the oil and lemon juice mixture and cook under a preheated broiler for about 10 minutes, basting frequently with the lemon and oil. Serve garnished with lemons and parsley.

The Basilica of St Paul's, Rome.

SERVES 4

Pasta Shells with Seafood

There are few Italian provinces which do not border on the sea, and seafood therefore plays an important part in the Italian diet, providing much needed protein.

PREPARATION TIME: 5 minutes
COOKING TIME: 15 minutes

9oz package pasta shells
1lb shrimp, shelled and deveined
¼lb scallops, cleaned and sliced
4 tbsps butter or margarine
2 cloves garlic, minced
½ cup dry white wine

1 cup cream
2 tbsps water
1 tbsp cornstarch
1 tbsp lemon juice
1 tbsp chopped parsley
Salt and pepper

Melt butter in a pan. Add garlic, and cook for 1 minute. Add wine and cream, bring back to boil, and cook 2 minutes. Slake corn starch with the water, and pour into sauce. Stir until boiling. Add lemon juice and salt and pepper to taste. Meanwhile, cook the pasta in plenty of boiling salted water, until tender – about 10 minutes. Drain, shaking to remove excess water. Add shrimp and scallops to sauce and cook 3 minutes. Pour the sauce over the pasta shells, toss, and garnish with parsley.

Above: the old town of Scilla, in the region of Calabria, perches near the tip of the boot of Italy. Right: Italy's Dolomite Mountains are easily accessible and many of the old roads built during the First World War are still in use today.

SERVES 4

Fish Stew

Gasps of delight will greet the presentation of this impressive dish.

PREPARATION TIME: 15 minutes
COOKING TIME: 35 minutes

1 medium-sized onion, finely
    chopped
2 cloves garlic, peeled and minced
3 tbsps olive oil
1½lbs tomatoes, skinned, seeded
    and chopped
2 tbsps tomato paste
2 cups dry red wine
Salt and freshly ground black
    pepper to taste

1 quart mussels in their shells,
    scrubbed
8 jumbo shrimp
½ cup peeled shrimp
4 crab claws, partly shelled

TO SERVE
8 small slices stale, crusty bread
A little olive oil
1 large clove garlic
Chopped parsley

Fry the onion gently in the olive oil for 3 minutes. Add the garlic and chopped tomatoes and fry gently for a further 3 minutes. Add the tomato paste and red wine and bring to the boil; simmer for 15 minutes. Add the mussels and simmer, covered, for 5 minutes. Add the jumbo shrimp, peeled shrimp and crab claws, and simmer for a further 5 minutes. Meanwhile, prepare the bread croûtes. Brush the slices of bread with a little olive oil and rub with the minced clove of garlic. Broil until crisp and golden and then sprinkle with chopped parsley. Spoon the fish stew into a deep serving dish and top with the bread croûtes. Serve immediately.

Facing page: the floodlit drama of the Cathedral of Santa Maria del Fiore in Florence.

SERVES 4

Crespelle with Tuna

Italian crespelles can be filled with a whole variety of ingredients.
Crespelles with tuna and tomato sauce make an excellent lunch dish.

PREPARATION TIME: 40 minutes
COOKING TIME: 30 minutes

12 CRESPELLE
3 eggs
¾ cup flour
Pinch of salt
1 cup water
½ tbsp olive oil
2 tbsps butter or margarine, melted

FILLING
1 cup tuna fish, drained
3 tbsps mayonnaise
1 tbsp tomato paste

TOMATO SAUCE
2 small cans (about 2 cups) tomato
    sauce
½ tsp basil
1 clove garlic, minced
1 onion, peeled and chopped
1 tbsp butter or margarine
2 tbsps chopped parsley
Salt
Pepper

To make crespelle
Sift the flour with a pinch of salt. Break eggs into a bowl and whisk. Add flour gradually, whisking all the time, until the mixture is smooth. Stir in water and mix the oil in well. Cover bowl with a damp cloth, and leave in a cool place for 30 minutes. Heat a crêpe pan or a 7-inch frying pan. Grease lightly with melted butter, and put a good tablespoon of batter in the center. Roll the pan to coat the surface evenly. Fry until crespelle is brown on the underside. Loosen edge with a spatula; turn over and brown on the other side. Stack and wrap in a clean cloth until needed.

To make sauce
Melt butter in pan and gently fry garlic and basil for 30 seconds. Add onion and fry until transparent. Add tomato sauce and cook for 10 minutes. Add salt and freshly-ground black pepper to taste, and parsley if desired.

To make filling
Flake tuna fish, and put into a bowl. Mix mayonnaise and tomato paste, and stir into tuna fish. Divide mixture equally between crespelle, placing mixture at one end and rolling up. Place in an ovenproof dish. Pour over tomato sauce, and cook under a broiler for 5 minutes. Serve immediately.

The warm, clear blue waters around Sorrento attract locals and tourists alike to the bathing jetty.

40

SERVES 4-6

Sherrie's Pizza

The variety of pizza toppings is endless. This recipe is particularly tasty but why not use your imagination to create your own favorites.

PREPARATION TIME: 40 minutes
COOKING TIME: 30-40 minutes

Pizza dough (see recipe for Pizza Rustica)
1½ cups chopped tomato pulp
½lb chopped, sliced mushrooms
Black and green olives

½lb pepperoni sausage, sliced
1 small green pepper, seeded and chopped
1 cup shredded mozarella cheese
¼ cup shredded Parmesan cheese

On a greased cookie sheet, stretch out dough large enough to make a 10-inch round. Pinch edge to make a rim. Cover with chopped tomato pulp, mushrooms, olives, sausage and chopped pepper. Sprinkle over mozarella and Parmesan. Bake in a preheated oven at 400°F for 30-40 minutes. Serve piping hot from the oven.

Venice's maze of small canals and bridges does much to enhance the city's romantic image.

SERVES 4

Farfalle with Beef, Mushroom and Soured Cream

Pasta butterflies combine beautifully with a rich, creamy sauce and tender succulent beef.

PREPARATION TIME: 10 minutes

COOKING TIME: 15 minutes

9oz package farfalle (pasta
  butterflies – bows)
½lb sirloin or butt steak, sliced
¾ cup mushrooms, sliced
¼ cup soured cream
10 green olives, pitted and
  chopped
1 onion, peeled and sliced

2 tbsps unsalted butter
1 tbsp flour
Salt and pepper

GARNISH
Soured cream
1 tbsp chopped parsley

With a very sharp knife, cut meat into narrow, short strips. Heat half the butter, and fry meat over a high heat until well browned. Set aside. Heat remaining butter in pan, and gently fry onion until soft and just beginning to color. Add mushrooms, and cook for 3 minutes. Stir in flour and continue frying for a further 3 minutes. Gradually stir in soured cream. When fully incorporated, add meat, olives, and salt and pepper to taste. Meanwhile, cook farfalle in plenty of boiling salted water for 10 minutes, or until tender but still firm. Drain well. Serve with beef and mushroom sauce on top. Garnish with a little extra soured cream and chopped parsley.

The ancient Roman Forum stands in the middle of some of the busiest streets in modern-day Rome.

SERVES 4

Pastitsio

A classic Italian bake which is ideal served as a warming winter meal.

PREPARATION TIME: 10 minutes

COOKING TIME: 1 hour

9oz package macaroni
4 tbsps butter or margarine
¼ cup Parmesan cheese, shredded
Pinch of shredded nutmeg
2 eggs, beaten
1 medium-sized onion, peeled and
    chopped
1 clove garlic, minced
1lb ground beef

2 tbsps tomato paste
¼ cup red wine
½ cup beef stock
2 tbsps chopped parsley
2 tbsps all-purpose flour
½ cup milk
Salt
Pepper

Set oven to 375°F. Cook macaroni in plenty of boiling salted water for 10 minutes, or until tender but still firm. Rinse under hot water. Drain. Put one-third of the butter in the pan and return macaroni to it. Add half the cheese, nutmeg, and salt and pepper to taste. Leave to cool. Mix in half the beaten egg, and put aside. Melt half of the remaining butter in a pan, and fry onion and garlic gently until onion is soft. Increase temperature, add meat, and fry until browned. Add tomato paste, stock, parsley and wine, and season with salt and pepper. Simmer for 20 minutes. In a small pan, melt the rest of the butter. Stir in the flour and cook for 30 seconds. Remove from heat, and stir in milk. Bring to boil, stirring continuously, until the sauce thickens. Beat in the remaining egg and season to taste. Spoon half the macaroni into a serving dish and cover with the meat sauce. Put on another layer of macaroni and smooth over. Pour over white sauce, sprinkle with remaining cheese, and bake in the oven for 30 minutes until golden brown. Serve immediately.

Left: the harbor at Marina Grande, on the island of Capri.

The spectacular beauty of Italy's Dolomite Mountains makes them a popular destination for visitors all year round.

SERVES 4

Whole-wheat Spaghetti with Walnuts and Parsley

Highly nutritious and tasty, this simple Italian dish is perfect for a family lunch.

PREPARATION TIME: 10 minutes
COOKING TIME: 10 minutes

9oz package whole-wheat
spaghetti
4 tbsps parsley
2 tbsps walnuts
¼ cup olive oil

2 cloves garlic, peeled
Salt and pepper
¼ cup shredded Parmesan or
pecorino cheese

Fry garlic gently in oil for 2 minutes. Set oil aside to cool. Wash parsley and remove stalks. Finely chop parsley, walnuts and garlic in a food processor with a metal blade, or in a blender. When chopped well, add cooled oil in a thin stream. Turn mixture into a bowl, mix in shredded cheese, and add salt and pepper to taste. Cook spaghetti in a large pan of boiling salted water for 10 minutes or until tender but still firm. Drain. Serve with sauce tossed through. Serve with a side dish of shredded Parmesan or pecorino cheese.

SERVES 4
Penne with Anchovy Sauce

Classic Italian ingredients enhance the flavor of the anchovies in this delicious recipe.

PREPARATION TIME: 5 minutes
COOKING TIME: 20 minutes

9oz package penne
6-8 anchovies
2 small cans (about 2 cups) tomato sauce
2 tbsps olive oil

3 tbsps chopped parsley
¼ cup Parmesan cheese, shredded
2 tbsps butter or margarine
Pepper

Chop anchovies and cook them in the oil, stirring to a paste. Add tomato sauce to anchovies, with parsley and freshly-ground black pepper to taste. Bring to the boil and simmer, uncovered, for 10 minutes. Meanwhile, cook the penne in lots of boiling salted water for 10 minutes, or until tender but still firm. Rinse in hot water and drain well. Toss in butter. Combine sauce with the pasta, sprinkle with parsley, and serve immediately with Parmesan cheese.

Right: the view down the Grand Canal from Venice's Rialto Bridge.

Pisa's Romanesque cathedral with the famous leaning tower in the background.

SERVES 4

Tagliatelle Carbonara

This quick pasta dish makes an ideal lunch or supper treat.

PREPARATION TIME: 10 minutes
COOKING TIME: 15 minutes

9oz package tagliatelle
2 tbsps butter or margarine
8 strips bacon, shredded
1 tbsp olive oil
⅓ cup cream

Pinch of paprika
¼ cup Parmesan cheese, shredded
2 eggs
Salt and pepper

Heat oil in a frying pan, add bacon and cook over a moderate heat until browning. Add paprika and cook for 1 minute. Add cream and stir. Beat together eggs and shredded cheese. Meanwhile, cook tagliatelle in lots of boiling salted water for 10 minutes, or until tender but still firm. Drain, return to pan with butter and black pepper and toss. Add bacon mixture and egg mixture, and toss together. Add salt to taste. Serve immediately.

Spinach and Fontina Cheese Lasagne

Spinach and cheese blend beautifully in this extra-special lasagne.

PREPARATION TIME: 20-25 minutes

COOKING TIME: 35 minutes

1lb cooked and drained spinach
(or thawed frozen spinach)
Generous pinch shredded nutmeg
Salt and freshly ground black
pepper to taste
2 tbsps cream
1 clove garlic, peeled and minced
1 egg yolk
1¼ cups fontina cheese, crumbled

8oz green or whole-wheat lasagre
(the non pre-cook variety)

SAUCE
½ cup cream
1 egg, beaten
2 tbsps shredded Parmesan cheese
3 firm tomatoes, sliced

Mix the cooked spinach with nutmeg and salt and pepper to taste; stir in the cream, garlic, egg yolk and crumbled fontina cheese. Layer the lasagne and spinach mixture in a lightly greased ovenproof dish, starting with spinach and finishing with lasagne. For the sauce: mix the cream with the beaten egg and half the shredded Parmesan cheese; spoon over the lasagne. Top with the sliced tomato and the remaining Parmesan cheese. Bake in the oven at 375°F for about 35 minutes, until golden. Serve piping hot.

Chickpea, Mint and Orange Salad

Salads need not be ordinary. This imaginative mixture is both refreshing and delicious.

PREPARATION TIME: 15-25 minutes

3 cups dried chickpeas, soaked
overnight and cooked
2 tbsps chopped fresh mint
1 clove garlic, peeled and minced
Salt and freshly ground black
pepper to taste
Juice of 1 orange

Rind of 1 orange, cut into
matchstick strips
3 tbsps olive oil
Segments from 2 large oranges

GARNISH
Fresh mint leaves

Mix the chickpeas with half the chopped mint, garlic, and salt and pepper to taste. Mix the orange juice, strips of orange rind and olive oil together; stir into the chickpeas. Lightly mix in the orange segments and garnish with the remaining chopped mint.

SERVES 4-6

Pizza Rustica

This farmhouse pie is really a cross between quiche and pizza. Whichever you think it resembles most, there is no question that it is delicious.

PREPARATION TIME: 40 minutes
COOKING TIME: 35 minutes

PIZZA DOUGH
½oz fresh yeast
½ tsp sugar
¾ cup lukewarm water
2 cups all-purpose flour
Pinch salt
2 tbsps oil

FILLING
Shredded Parmesan cheese
4oz prosciutto or Parma ham,
  sliced
2 tomatoes, peeled, seeded and
  roughly chopped
2oz mozzarella cheese, diced
1 tbsp chopped fresh parsley
1 tbsp chopped fresh basil
2 eggs, lightly beaten
5 tbsps heavy cream
2oz fontina cheese, finely shredded
Pinch nutmeg
Salt and pepper

Cream the yeast with the sugar in a small bowl, add the lukewarm water and leave to stand for 10 minutes to prove. Bubbles will appear on the surface when ready. Sift flour and salt into a bowl, make a well in the center and add the oil and the yeast mixture. Using a wooden spoon, beat the liquid in the center of the well, gradually incorporating the flour from the outside until it forms a firm dough. Turn the dough out onto a floured surface and knead for 10 minutes, or until the dough is smooth and elastic. Place in a lightly oiled bowl or in a large plastic bag, cover or tie the bag and leave to stand in a warm place for 30 minutes, or until the dough has doubled in bulk.

Knock the dough back and knead it into a smooth ball. Flatten the dough and roll out into a circle on a floured surface. The circle should be about 10 inches in diameter. Lightly oil the baking dish, place in the dough and press out with floured fingertips to form a raised edge on the sides of the dish. Sprinkle the base of the dough with some of the Parmesan cheese and place on a layer of ham. Cover the ham with the chopped tomato. Mix the remaining ingredients together and pour over the tomato and ham.

Bake on the lowest shelf of the oven for about 35 minutes at 375°F. The top of the pizza should be nicely browned and the edge of the dough should be golden when the pizza is ready. Serve hot.

SERVES 4

Lasagne

One taste of a home-made lasagne will be enough to convince the most dedicated couch potato to give up TV dinners.

PREPARATION TIME: 10 minutes

COOKING TIME: 45 minutes

8 lasagne noodles

MEAT SAUCE
4 tbsps butter or margarine
1 carrot, diced
1 celery stick, diced
1 onion, peeled and diced
¼lb ground beef
1 tsp marjoram
1 tbsp flour
1 tbsp tomato paste
½ cup beef stock
Salt
Pepper

BÉCHAMEL SAUCE
2 tbsps butter or margarine
2 tbsps flour
1 cup milk
6 peppercorns
1 bay leaf
Slice of onion
Parsley stalks

To make meat sauce

Heat the butter in a pan and add onion, celery and carrot. Cook until the onion is golden. Add ground beef and brown well. Stir in flour; add tomato paste, beef stock, marjoram, and salt and pepper. Cook for 15 minutes.

Meanwhile, cook the lasagne in lots of boiling salted water for 10 minutes, or until tender. Rinse in cold water and drain carefully. Lay out on a clean cloth to dry.

To make béchamel sauce

Heat milk in a saucepan with peppercorns, slice of onion, bay leaf and parsley stalks. Bring to simmering point and remove from heat. Allow to cool for 5 minutes. Strain. Melt butter in a saucepan. Stir in flour and cook for 30 seconds. Remove from heat and gradually add milk, stirring continuously. Cook for 3 minutes.

Grease an ovenproof baking dish. Line base with a layer of lasagne sheets. Cover with a layer of meat sauce, and a layer of béchamel sauce. Place another layer of lasagne, repeating until all the ingredients are used, finishing with a layer of lasagne and a layer of béchamel sauce. Bake in oven at 400°F until the top is golden. Serve immediately.

Facing page bottom: Rome's Colosseum, begun by Vespasian in A.D. 75.

*Florence's magnificent cathedral with the Romanesque baptistry
of San Giovanni, in the left foreground.*

SERVES 4

Spaghetti Bolognese

A classic Italian dish which tastes delicious and is great fun to eat.

PREPARATION TIME: 10 minutes
COOKING TIME: 1 hour 15 minutes

9oz package spaghetti
2 tbsps butter or margarine
1 tbsp olive oil
2 onions, peeled and chopped
   finely
½lb ground beef
1 carrot, scraped and chopped
   finely

¼ cup tomato paste
1 cup brown stock
2 tbsps sherry
Salt and pepper
Parmesan cheese, shredded

Heat the butter and oil in a pan and fry the onions and carrot slowly until soft. Increase heat and add the ground beef. Fry for a few minutes, then stir, cooking until meat is browned all over. Add the tomato paste, salt and pepper to taste, and the stock, and simmer gently for about ¾ hour, stirring occasionally, until the mixture thickens. Add 2 tablespoons sherry, and cook for a further 5 minutes. Meanwhile, place the spaghetti in lots of boiling salted water, and cook for 10 minutes, or until tender but still firm. Drain. Serve with Bolognese sauce on top, and sprinkle with Parmesan cheese.

SERVES 4

Home-made Tagliatelle with Summer Sauce

Pasta making is not as difficult as you might think. It is well worth it, too, because home-made pasta is in a class by itself.

PREPARATION TIME: 30 minutes plus overnight refrigeration

COOKING TIME: 5-6 minutes

PASTA DOUGH
1 cup all-purpose flour
1 cup bread flour
2 large eggs
2 tsps olive oil
Pinch salt

SAUCE
1lb unpeeled tomatoes, seeded and
    cut into small dice
1 large green pepper, cored, seeded
    and cut in small dice
1 onion, cut into small dice
1 tbsps chopped fresh basil
1 tbsp chopped fresh parsley
2 cloves garlic, minced
½ cup olive oil and vegetable oil
    mixed

Place the flours in a mound on a work surface and make a well in the center. Place the eggs, oil and salt in the center of the well. Using a fork, beat the ingredients in the center to blend them and gradually incorporate the flour from the outside edge. The dough may also be mixed in a food processor. When half the flour is incoporated, start kneading using the palms of the hands and not the fingers. This may also be done in a food processor. Cover the dough and leave it to rest for 15 minutes.

Divide the dough in quarters and roll out thinly with a rolling pin on a floured surface or use a pasta machine, dusting dough lightly with flour before rolling. If using a machine, follow the manufacturer's directions. Allow the sheets of pasta to dry for about 10 minutes on a floured surface or on tea towels. Cut the sheets into strips about ¼-inch wide by hand or machine, dusting lightly with flour while cutting. Leave the cut pasta to dry while preparing the sauce.

Combine all the sauce ingredients, mixing well. Cover and refrigerate overnight.

Cook the pasta for 5-6 minutes in boiling salted water with a spoonful of oil. Drain the pasta and rinse under very hot water. Toss in a colander to drain excess water. Place the hot pasta in serving dish. Pour the cold sauce over and toss.

The popular resort of Marina Grande on the island of Capri.

SERVES 4
Pasta Shells with Gorgonzola Cheese Sauce

Gorgonzola is now widely available in supermarkets, alongside an ever-increasing variety of Italian cheeses.

PREPARATION TIME: 5 minutes
COOKING TIME: 15 minutes

½lb gorgonzola cheese
⅓ cup milk
2 tbsps butter or margarine
3 tbsps heavy cream

9oz package pasta shells
Salt
Parmesan cheese, shredded

Heat gorgonzola cheese, milk and butter gently, in a pan. Stir to a sauce with a wooden spoon. Stir in cream. Add salt if necessary. Meanwhile, cook shells in plenty of boiling salted water for 10 1⁄4inutes, or until shells are tender but still firm. Drain, shaking colander to remove excess water. Add shells to hot sauce and toss to coat well. Serve immediately with shredded Parmesan cheese on the side.

Right: the shop-lined Rialto Bridge in Venice crosses the Grand Canal.

Tagliatelle with Garlic and Oil

SERVES 3-4

Garlic finds its way into a great many Italian dishes and this one in particular is a garlic-lovers delight.

PREPARATION TIME: 5 minutes

COOKING TIME: 10 minutes

9oz package green tagliatelle	2 tbsps chopped parsley
½ cup olive oil	Salt and pepper
3 cloves garlic, minced	

Cook the tagliatelle in lots of boiling salted water for 10 minutes, or until tender but still firm, stirring occasionally. Meanwhile, make the sauce. Heat the oil in a pan and, when warm, add peeled, minced garlic. Fry gently until golden brown. Add chopped parsley, and salt and pepper to taste. Drain tagliatelle. Add sauce and toss to coat well. Serve hot.

Spaghetti with Basil Sauce (Pesto)

SERVES 3-4

This simple yet stylish dish is a good alternative to rich and creamy dishes such as Lasagne.

PREPARATION TIME: 5 minutes

COOKING TIME: 15 minutes

9oz package spaghetti	3 tbsps Parmesan or pecorino
2 cups fresh basil leaves	cheese, shredded
2 tbsps pine nuts	
¼ cup olive oil	**GARNISH**
2 cloves garlic, peeled	Fresh basil
Salt and pepper	

Wash basil and remove leaves, discarding stems. Heat 1 tbsp of oil over a low temperature. Add garlic and pine nuts, and cook until pine nuts are a light golden brown. Drain. Finely chop basil leaves, pine nuts and garlic in a food processor with a metal blade, or in a blender. When smooth, add remaining oil in a thin stream, blending continuously. Turn mixture into a bowl; mix in cheese, and add salt and pepper to taste. Meanwhile, cook spaghetti in a large pan of boiling salted water for 10 minutes, or until just tender. Drain, and serve with basil sauce tossed through. Serve with side dish of shredded cheese. Garnish with fresh basil.

The clear seas and rugged scenery of Amalfi, on the Sorrento Peninsula, make it one of the most beautiful resorts in Italy.

SERVES 4

Pasta Spirals with Kidneys in Madeira Sauce

This unusual combination is very healthful and appetizing – perfect for a filling family meal.

PREPARATION TIME: 15 minutes

COOKING TIME: 30 minutes

9oz package pasta spirals
6 lambs' kidneys
1 tbsp flour
Salt and pepper
1 small onion, peeled and chopped finely

1 clove garlic, minced
4 tbsps butter or margarine
¾ cup mushrooms, sliced
6 strips bacon, diced
½ cup Madeira wine, or dry white wine

Split and remove hard core from kidneys. Cut in half lengthwise. Add salt and pepper to flour and mix well. Coat kidneys in seasoned flour. Heat butter in pan; add onion and garlic, and cook until soft and translucent. Add kidneys and brown on both sides. Add bacon and mushroom, and cook, stirring frequently, for 3 minutes. Add wine, and bring to the boil. Simmer gently for 15 minutes, or until kidneys are tender. Adjust seasoning. Meanwhile, cook the pasta spirals in plenty of boiling salted water for 10 minutes, or until tender but still firm. Rinse in hot water and drain well. Serve immediately with kidney sauce on top.

The ruins of Hadrian's Villa at Tivoli, near Rome; in Roman times the town was a great favorite with nobles and emperors.

SERVES 4

Spaghetti with Egg, Bacon and Mushroom

This dish is the perfect answer when you require a quick, tasty meal.

PREPARATION TIME: 10 minutes
COOKING TIME: 15 minutes

9oz package spaghetti
1 cup mushrooms, sliced
4 strips bacon, diced
4 tbsps butter or margarine
¼ cup Parmesan cheese, shredded

2 eggs, hard-cooked and chopped finely
1 tbsp chopped parsley
Salt and pepper

Melt half the butter in a frying pan. Add mushrooms and bacon, and cook for 10 minutes over a moderate heat, until the bacon is crisp. Meanwhile, cook the spaghetti in lots of boiling salted water until tender but still firm – about 10 minutes. Drain. Return to pan. Add rest of butter, salt, and lots of freshly-ground black pepper, and the mushrooms and bacon. Toss together. Serve with hard-cooked eggs sprinkled on top, and parsley if desired. Serve shredded Parmesan cheese separately.

SERVES 4

Brasciole with Tagliatelle

Veal steaks are rolled with slices of ham to create this rich and unusual dish.

PREPARATION TIME: 15 minutes

COOKING TIME: 25 minutes

½lb tagliatelle
4 veal steaks, or cutlets
4 thin slices ham
4 tbsps shredded Parmesan cheese
2 tbsps butter or margarine

2 small cans (about 2 cups) tomato
 sauce
Salt
Pepper

Pound veal steaks out thinly. Place a slice of ham on the top of each steak. Sprinkle a tablespoon of the Parmesan cheese over each steak, and freshly-ground black pepper. Roll up, and tie gently with string at each end and in the middle. Heat butter in a pan, and add veal rolls. Cook gently until lightly browned all over. Add tomato sauce, and cover. Cook for 15 minutes. Meanwhile, cook tagliatelle in plenty of boiling salted water for 10 minutes, or until tender but still firm. Rinse in hot water, and drain. Cut veal rolls into 1-inch rounds. Toss tagliatelle together with tomato sauce, and top with veal rolls and shredded Parmesan cheese. Serve immediately.

Left: a spectacular view from the Villa Rufolo along the Sorrento peninsula at Ravello.

73

SERVES 4

Roast Pork Fillet with Rosemary

The simple addition of rosemary is enough to bring out all the flavor of the pork in this delicious dish.

PREPARATION TIME: 15 minutes
COOKING TIME: 45 minutes

1¼lbs pork fillet
2 cloves garlic, chopped
½ tsp coarse sea salt
Few leaves tarragon

Rectangular strip of pork fat
1 sprig rosemary, chopped
1 tbsp oil
Pepper

Spread out the fat and sprinkle over the garlic, rosemary, sea salt, pepper and tarragon. Place the fillet in the center of the prepared fat and roll the fat around the meat. Secure with kitchen string. Brush an ovenproof dish with oil, place in the pork fillet and roast in a hot oven for 45 minutes, turning the pork over once, halfway through cooking. Serve either hot or cold, cut into thick slices with the cooking juices spooned over.

For the gondoliers of Venice, summertime means endless tourist trips around the city's waterways.

SERVES 4

Piquant Liver

Liver is a valuable ingredient in a healthful diet. Here it is enhanced with wine and served simply, with rice.

PREPARATION TIME: 15 minutes

COOKING TIME: 20 minutes

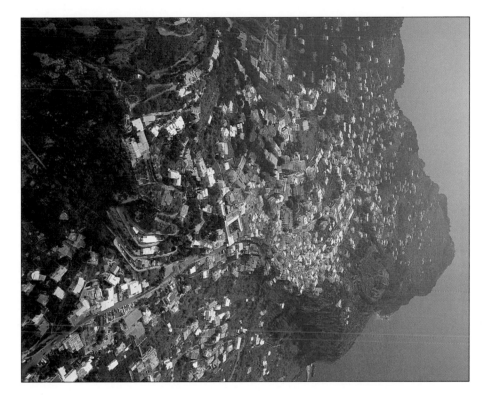

1lb liver, cut into thin strips	1 tbsp flour
4 tbsps butter or margarine	Salt
2 tbsps wine vinegar	Pepper
1 onion, peeled and finely sliced	
⅓ cup white wine	**GARNISH**
1 tbsp chopped parsley	Chopped parsley

Combine flour with a good pinch of salt and freshly-ground black pepper. Toss in liver and coat well. Heat frying pan and add half the butter over a gentle heat. Add onion and fry gently until transparent. Add vinegar and cook over high heat until vinegar has evaporated. Add remaining butter and when hot, add liver. Fry quickly for about 3 minutes. Add wine, parsley, and salt and pepper to taste. Bring to the boil and simmer for 5 minutes. Sprinkle with chopped parsley and serve with rice.

Above: rugged limestone crags are characteristic of the tiny island of Capri – as is the development which goes with tourism!

SERVES 4-6

Chicken in Sweet-Sour Sauce

"Pollo in dolce-forte" is not a Chinese dish but an authentic Italian dish, given its sweet-sour flavor by the addition of juniper berries and maraschino liqueur.

PREPARATION TIME: 2-3 hours marinating time
COOKING TIME: 1 hour

1 chicken weighing about 4lbs	5 tbsps white wine vinegar
1 large onion	10 tbsps water
1 large carrot	1 bay leaf
15 juniper berries	4 tbsp olive oil
5 tbsps maraschino liqueur	Salt and pepper

Joint the chicken. Marinate for several hours in the chopped onion, carrot, liqueur, vinegar, and water, juniper berries and bay leaf. Take the joints from the marinade, drain well. Saute in the olive oil until golden. Place in a shallow casserole, add the unstrained marinade, cover and cook at 300°F for about 1 hour or until the chicken is tender. Place on a warmed serving platter and keep warm. Remove the bay leaf and press the cooking juices through a sieve. Reheat gently and pour over the chicken to serve.

The Neptune Fountain in the Piazza della Signoria, Florence.

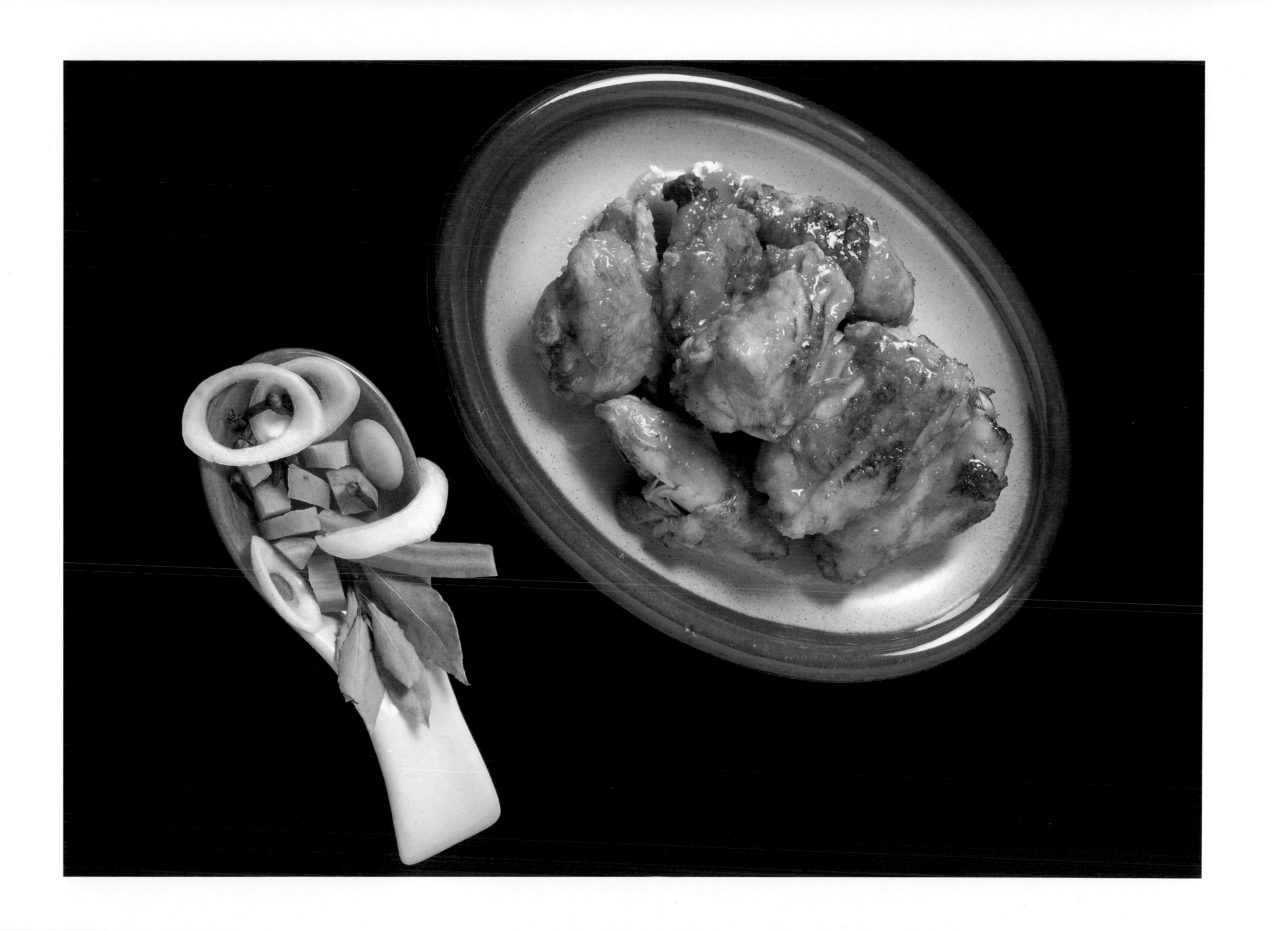

SERVES 4

Veal Chops with Wine

Veal is extremely popular in Italy, where it is used in a variety of delicious dishes.

PREPARATION TIME: 30 minutes
COOKING TIME: 1 hour 20 minutes

4 veal chops
3 tbsps flour
Salt and pepper
2 tbsps oil

1 onion, chopped
1 cup mushrooms, left whole
1 cup white wine

Trim chops and coat with seasoned flour. Heat oil and brown the chops on both sides, then transfer to a casserole dish. Add onion to remaining oil and cook till lightly brown. Add remaining flour and mix well. Add mushrooms and wine and bring to boiling point, stirring all the time. Pour sauce over chops in the casserole. Cover and cook for about 1 hour at 350°F.

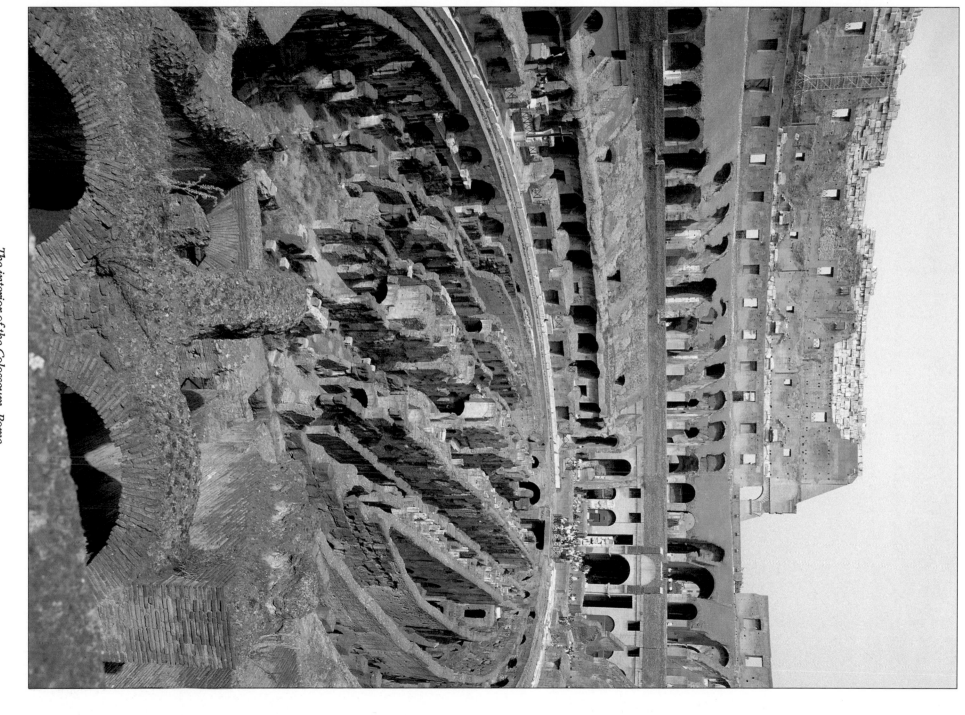

The interior of the Colosseum, Rome.

SERVES 4

Winter Salami Risotto

The wonderful combination of textures in this dish make it the perfect choice for a special lunch or supper dish.

PREPARATION TIME: 10 minutes
COOKING TIME: 12 minutes

8oz salami, thinly sliced
4-6oz assorted cured Italian meats
2 green peppers
1 red pepper
4 large, ripe tomatoes

½ cup green beans, cooked
8 stuffed olives
2 cups medium or long grain rice, cooked
3-4 tbsps Italian dressing

Chop some of the meats and roll the remainder. Chop most of the vegetables, leaving a few large pieces for garnish. Slice the stuffed olives. Blend the rice with the dressing, chopped meat, vegetables and olives and put in the bottom of a shallow dish. Top with the larger pieces of vegetables and rolls of meat. Serve with a green salad.

Facing page: pleasure craft now outnumber fishing boats in many of Italy's coastal villages.

SERVES 4-6

Turkey Salad

Serve this unusual salad for a special summer lunch or in small portions as an appetizer.

PREPARATION TIME: 20 minutes
COOKING TIME: 4-5 minutes

1 Romaine lettuce	Salt and freshly ground black
Few young spinach leaves	pepper to taste
Juice of 1 lemon	1 egg
6 tbsps olive oil	2 slices bread, cut into small cubes
2 cloves garlic, peeled and minced	6oz cooked turkey, cut into thin
3 drops Tabasco	strips
4 anchovies, chopped	

Tear the lettuce into pieces and put into a salad bowl with the young spinach leaves. Mix the lemon juice with 3 tbsps of the olive oil, half the garlic, Tabasco, anchovies and salt and pepper to taste. Put the egg into a pan of boiling water and cook for just 45 seconds – the white and yolk must still be very runny. Carefully crack the egg and scoop all the center egg into the dressing; beat well. Heat the remaining olive oil with the rest of the garlic in a large, shallow pan; add the small cubes of bread and fry until crisp and golden. Add the croûtons, turkey strips and prepared dressing to the salad greens and toss well together. Serve immediately.

Above: the cathedral and campanile in St Mark's Square, Venice.

SERVES 4

Chicken Liver Risotto with Red Beans

Packed full of goodness and taste, this dish is a positive health bonus.

PREPARATION TIME: 15 minutes
COOKING TIME: 25-30 minutes

1 medium-sized onion, finely
   chopped
2 tbsps olive oil
1 clove garlic, peeled and minced
1½ cups brown or wild rice
2½ cups chicken stock
Salt and freshly ground black
   pepper to taste

8oz chicken livers, chopped
2 tbsps butter
6oz cooked red kidney beans
1 tbsp chopped parsley

Fry the onion gently in the olive oil for 3 minutes. Add the garlic and the rice and stir over the heat for 1 minute, until the rice is evenly coated with oil. Gradually stir in the chicken stock. Bring to the boil and add salt and pepper to taste; cover and simmer for 20 minutes. Meanwhile, fry the chopped chicken livers in the butter for about 4 minutes until sealed on the outside but still pink in the center. Drain the chicken livers with a slotted spoon and stir into the cooked rice together with the red kidney beans and chopped parsley. Heat through. Serve hot with shredded Parmesan cheese, if liked.

Left: the Ponte Vecchio, the oldest bridge in Florence, dates from 1345.

SERVES 4

Beef in Barolo

One of Italy's best-loved wines, Barolo makes this dish extra special, and the perfect centerpiece for an Italian-style dinner party.

PREPARATION TIME: 5 minutes plus overnight marinating

COOKING TIME: 2½-3 hours

2lbs tenderloin beef	2 tsps tomato paste
1 carrot, sliced	3 tbsps olive oil
1 onion, sliced	2 cloves garlic, minced
½ leek, sliced	1 bottle Barolo wine
1 bay leaf	2½ cups water or beef stock
1 sprig rosemary	Salt and pepper
1 sprig thyme	5 peppercorns

Mix together the carrot, onion, leek, thyme, rosemary, bay leaf, garlic, peppercorns, a little ground pepper, tomato paste and the wine. Add the meat and marinate overnight.

Drain the meat, heat the olive oil and seal the meat on all sides until lightly browned.

Tip out excess fat and deglaze with the marinade. Pour over the 2½ cups of water or beef stock. Season with salt and pepper and simmer gently for 2 hours. Test the meat for tenderness and continue cooking if necessary, adding more water if required.

Cut the beef into slices, strain the sauce and serve with the sauce poured over.

Above: colorful buildings line the beach at San Terenzo, Levante.

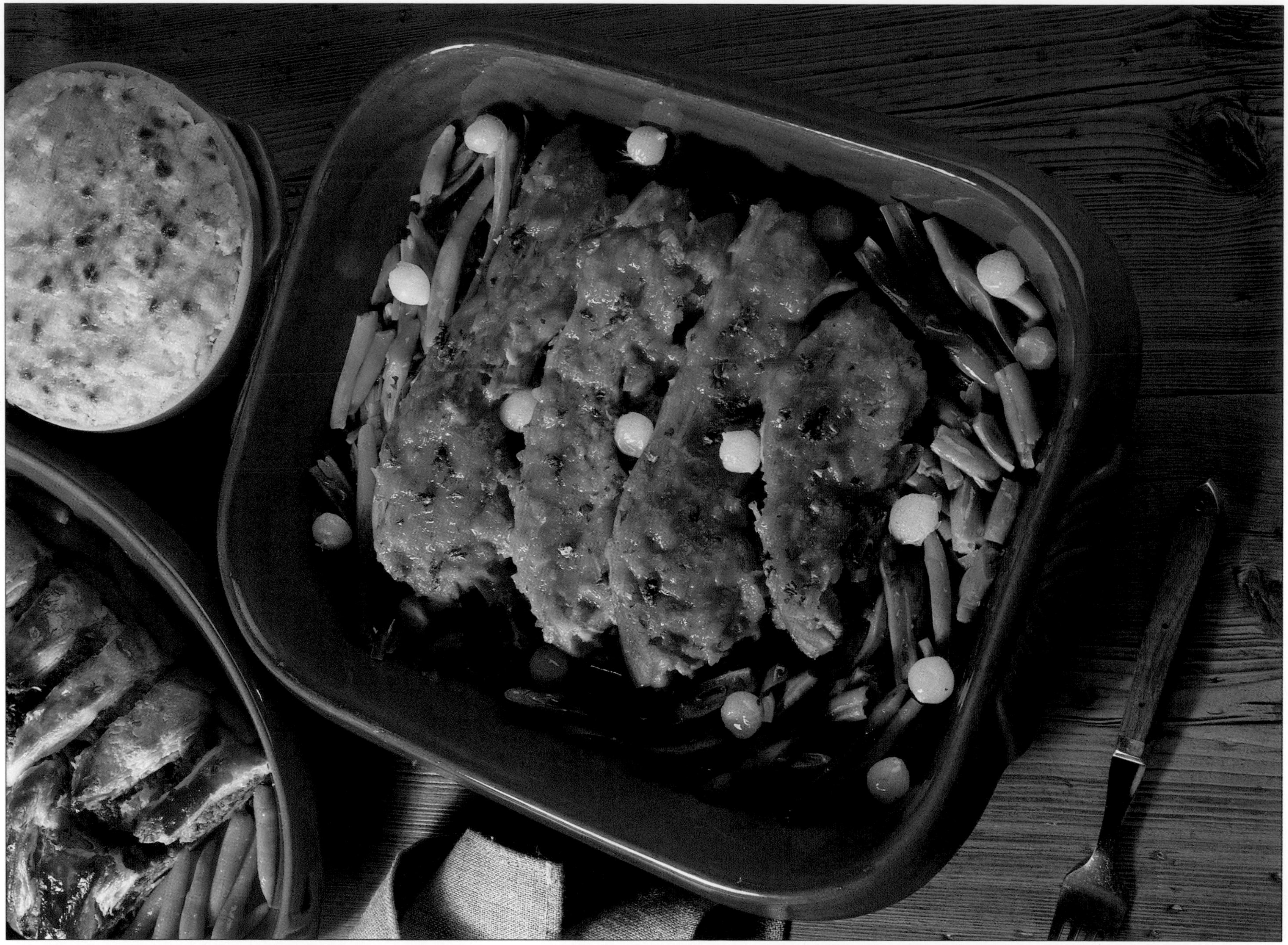

SERVES 4

Veal Cutlets with Vegetables

Veal is greatly enhanced by the addition of Marsala – a dessert wine from Sicily. If you cannot obtain any, sherry will serve as a substitute.

PREPARATION TIME: 5 minutes
COOKING TIME: 30 minutes

4 veal cutlets	8oz green beans, sliced
Salt and pepper	1 cup shallots
2 tbsps flour	¼ cup Marsala
4 tbsps clarified butter, or butter	½ cup chicken stock
and oil mixed	1 tbsp chopped parsley

Sprinkle the veal cutlets with salt and pepper and dredge with flour. Heat the butter, or butter and oil, in a frying pan and gently fry the cutlets on both sides for a few minutes. Lower the heat, add the stock and cook, covered, until tender. Add the shallots halfway through the cooking time. Meanwhile, cook the beans in boiling water for about 5-8 minutes. Drain and keep warm. Remove the meat and shallots and add the Marsala. Bring to the boil, stirring continuously. Arrange the cutlets on a serving dish, surrounded by the beans and shallots. Cover with the sauce and sprinkle with chopped parsley.

Above: the busy town of Messina was rebuilt in 1908 after an earthquake destroyed a large proportion of its houses.

SERVES 4

Lemon Chicken

The refreshing taste of lemon adds a subtle yet distinct flavor to the humble chicken.

PREPARATION TIME: 5 minutes
COOKING TIME: 40 minutes

2lbs chicken pieces
⅓ cup oil

LEMON SAUCE
Juice of 1 lemon
⅓ cup water
2 tsps cornstarch

2 tbsps sweet sherry
Pinch of sugar if desired

GARNISH
Lemon slices

Heat frying pan and add oil. When hot, add chicken pieces and toss in oil until well browned. Reduce heat and cover. Simmer for 30 minutes until chicken is cooked. Remove with a slotted spoon and drain on paper towels. Place chicken pieces in a serving dish and keep warm. Meanwhile, carefully drain oil from pan. Slake cornstarch in 2 tbsps of water. Put lemon juice and remaining water in pan, and bring to the boil. Add cornstarch and stir until boiling. Simmer for 2 minutes until thickened. Add sherry and sugar, and simmer a further 2 minutes. Pour over chicken pieces and garnish with lemon slices. Serve with boiled rice.

In Rome stands a statue of the city's legendary founders, Romulus and Remus, with their wolf foster mother.

SERVES 6-8
Risotto Milanese

An authentic Italian meal always includes a risotto. In Milan this delicious recipe is a particular favorite.

PREPARATION TIME: 10 minutes
COOKING TIME: 25-30 minutes

½ cup butter
2 tbsps chopped beef marrow
½ small onion, chopped
Salt and freshly ground pepper
½ cup dry white wine

2 cups rice
1 tsp crumbled saffron
4 cups (1 quart) chicken broth
½ cup shredded Parmesan Cheese

Melt half of the butter in a saucepan. Add beef marrow, onion and a pinch of salt and pepper. When onion is tender but not brown, add wine and let it boil until half its original volume. Stir in rice. Dissolve saffron in broth and add to pan. Stir to keep rice from sticking. When broth is simmering stir occasionally and cook until rice is cooked al dente and liquid is absorbed. Add more broth from time to time, if necessary, to prevent sticking. Stir in remaining butter and shredded Parmesan. Stand over very low heat for a few minutes before serving.

Above: the cathedral in Milan is of vast dimensions and is widely recognised as one of the world's most beautiful churches.

SERVES 4

Turkey Marsala

Marsala is a dessert-wine from Sicily which complements chicken, veal or turkey surprisingly well.

PREPARATION TIME: 25 minutes
COOKING TIME: 15 minutes

4 turkey breast fillets or escalopes
4 tbsps butter or margarine
1 clove garlic
4 anchovy fillets, soaked in milk
Capers
4 slices mozzarella cheese

2 tsps chopped marjoram
1 tbsp chopped parsley
3 tbsps Marsala
½ cup heavy cream
Salt and pepper

Flatten the turkey breasts between two sheets of wax paper with a meat mallet or rolling pin if necessary. Melt butter in a sauté pan and, when foaming, add the garlic and the turkey. Cook for a few minutes on each side until lightly browned. Remove them from the pan.

Drain the anchovy fillets and rinse them well. Dry on paper towels. Put a slice of cheese on top of each turkey fillet and arrange the anchovies and capers on top of each. Sprinkle with the chopped herbs and return the turkey to the pan. Cook the turkey a further 5 minutes over moderate heat, until the turkey is done and the cheese has melted. Remove to a serving dish and keep warm. Return the pan to the heat and add the Marsala. Scrape the browned pan juices off the bottom and reduce the heat. Add the cream and whisk in well. Lower the heat and simmer gently, uncovered, for a few minutes to thicken the sauce. Season the sauce with salt and pepper and spoon over the turkey fillets to serve.

The pretty town of Taormina sits high on a cliff on the east coast of Sicily.

SERVES 4

Zucchini, Caper and Anchovy Salad

Classic Italian ingredients unite to produce this marvellous summer salad.

PREPARATION TIME: 15-20 minutes

1lb zucchini
1 small onion, thinly sliced
1 tbsp capers
4-6 anchovies, chopped
1 tbsp anchovy oil (drained from
   the can of anchovies)
2 tbsps olive oil
2 tbsps tarragon vinegar

Juice of ½ lemon
Salt and freshly ground black
   pepper to taste

GARNISH
3 sprigs rosemary
2 whole anchovies

The secret of this salad is to slice the raw zucchini really thinly – you can do this with a sharp knife, but it is much easier if you use the slicing blade on a food processor or a mandolin. Trim the zucchini, and slice very thinly. Mix with the onion, capers and chopped anchovies. Mix the anchovy oil, olive oil, tarragon vinegar and lemon juice together; add salt and pepper to taste. Stir the dressing into the prepared salad ingredients and garnish with anchovies and rosemary.

Right: a trip in a gondola epitomizes the atmosphere of Venice for the many tourists who flock to the city every year.

SERVES 4

Black-eye Beans with Curry Dressing

Curry dressing adds extra flavor to this appetizing and healthful dish.

PREPARATION TIME: 10-15 minutes
COOKING TIME: 35-40 minutes

½lb black-eye beans, soaked overnight
Salt and freshly ground black pepper to taste
1 small onion, thinly sliced
1 green pepper, seeded and finely chopped
Juice of ½ lemon
2 tbsps cashew nuts, whole or roughly chopped

DRESSING
⅔ cup natural yogurt
2 tsps curry powder
2 tbsps fresh pineapple juice
1 clove garlic, minced

GARNISH
Curry powder

Simmer the beans in salted water until tender. Drain. Mix the black-eyed beans with the onion and green pepper. Stir in the lemon juice, salt and pepper to taste and the cashew nuts. For the dressing: mix all the ingredients together, adding salt and pepper to taste. Spoon the bean salad into a bowl, and spoon the prepared dressing over the top. Sprinkle with curry powder.

Above: the rugged coastline of Sorrento is dotted with small towns and fishing villages.

SERVES 4

Cheese Salad

Serve this exotic salad on a hot summer day – your guests will be delighted.

PREPARATION TIME: 10-12 minutes

½ a head of chicory
½ iceberg lettuce
1 cucumber, peeled and sliced
3-4 large tomatoes, cut into wedges, or 15-20 baby tomatoes, halved
8-10 pitted green or black olives, halved
1 medium-sized Spanish or red onion, peeled and chopped
1 cup mozzarella cheese, cut into ½-inch pieces

DRESSING
⅓ cup olive oil
2½ tbsps red wine vinegar
1½ tsps chopped fresh oregano or ½ tsp dried oregano
¾ tsp salt
½ tsp freshly ground black pepper
¾ tsp brown sugar

Wash and dry the chicory and lettuce leaves; tear into bite-size pieces. Place the chicory and lettuce in a large bowl and add the cucumber, tomatoes, olives, onion and cheese. Shake the dressing ingredients together in a screw-top jar. Pour the dressing over the salad. Toss lightly and serve.

The Spanish Steps – a beautiful Baroque staircase which leads to the church of the Santissima Trinà dei Monti, in Rome.

SERVES 4

Rice and Sole Salad

The mixture of fish, vegetables and herbs in this dish ensures an exotic and colorful result.

PREPARATION TIME: 30 minutes
COOKING TIME: 8-10 minutes

2 sole, filleted and skinned
4-6 peppercorns
Slice of onion
Lemon juice
5 tbsps olive oil
1 cup long-grain rice
1 red pepper
1 shallot, finely chopped
1 small eggplant

1 green pepper
2 bunches watercress
¼ cups prepared mayonnaise
1 clove garlic
1 level tsp tomato paste
1 level tsp paprika
1 tbsp chopped mixed herbs
Salt and pepper

Put the sole fillets into a baking dish. Add onion, a squeeze of lemon juice, peppercorns and enough water to cover. Sprinkle with salt, cover with buttered aluminum foil, and bake in oven at 350°F for about 8-10 minutes. Allow fish to cool in the liquid, then cut into 1-inch pieces. Cook rice for about 12 minutes. Drain under hot water, then cold, and leave to drain completely dry. Chop green and red peppers into ¼-inch dice. Cut eggplant in half lengthwise, score each half, sprinkle with salt, and leave to sit for about ½ hour. Wash eggplant well, then dry it. Cut it into ½-inch cubes and fry very quickly in 2 tbsps olive oil. Add salt and pepper, and toss with the cooked rice, and red and green pepper. Add a pinch of chopped herbs. Making a dressing with 1 tbsp lemon juice, 3 tbsps olive oil and shallot. Toss with the rice. Mince the clove of garlic and work it together with the mayonnaise, tomato paste and paprika. Add salt, pepper and the rest of the chopped herbs. Thin with a little milk or hot water. Adjust seasoning. Arrange rice salad on one side of serving dish, and put sole fillets on the other. Spoon mayonnaise dressing over fillets. Divide the two sides with bunches of watercress.

Above: the terracotta-colored rooftops of Florence, one of Italy's most fascinating and historically rich cities.

SERVES 4

Tuna Salad Naples Style

A wonderful mix of classic Italian ingredients makes this the perfect salad for a special summer picnic.

PREPARATION TIME: 20 minutes
COOKING TIME: 15-20 minutes

1 can tuna
4oz shrimp
6-8 anchovies
4 ripe tomatoes
4 hard-cooked eggs
1 red pepper
½ cup black olives, pitted

1 cup green beans
2 large potatoes, or 6 small new potatoes
2 tbsps white wine vinegar
6 tbsps olive oil
3 tbsps chopped mixed herbs
Salt and pepper

Peel and cook potatoes (skins may be left on new potatoes if desired) until tender. If using large potatoes, cut into ½-inch dice (new potatoes may be sliced into ¼-inch rounds). Trim beans, put into boiling salted water for about 3-4 minutes or until just barely cooked. Drain and rinse under cold water, then leave to drain dry. Cut the olives in half, lengthwise. Cut anchovies in half, lengthwise, then through the middle. Cut tomatoes into quarters (or eighths, if large) and remove the cores. Mix the vinegar and oil together for the vinaigrette dressing, and add seasoning and chopped herbs. Drain oil from tuna fish. Cut red pepper into thin shreds. Mix together all the ingredients, including the shrimp, and toss in the dressing. Quarter the eggs and toss into the other ingredients very carefully – do not break up the eggs. Pile onto dishes and serve.

Above left: as the third largest city in Italy, Naples has a large harbor which bustles with activity all year round. Above right: early morning near St Mark's Square, Venice.

Cortina d'Ampezzo is a popular resort for winter sports and hosted the Winter Olympics of 1956.

Sicilian Caponata

Vegetables, so important in Italian cuisine, are often served separately. This combination makes an excellent appetizer, vegetable course or accompaniment.

PREPARATION TIME: 35 minutes
COOKING TIME: 25-30 minutes

1 eggplant	1lb canned plum tomatoes
Salt	2 tbsps red wine vinegar
½ cup olive oil	1 tbsp sugar
1 onion, sliced	1 clove garlic, minced
2 sweet red peppers, cored, seeded	12 black olives, pitted
and cut into 1-inch pieces	1 tbsp capers
2 sticks celery, sliced thickly	Salt and pepper

Cut the eggplant in half and score the cut surface. Sprinkle with salt and leave to drain in a colander or on paper towels for 30 minutes. Rinse, pat dry and cut into 1-inch cubes.

Heat the oil in a large sauté pan and add the onion, peppers and celery. Lower the heat and cook for about 5 minutes, stirring occasionally. Add the eggplant and cook for a further 5 minutes. Sieve the tomatoes to remove the seeds and add the pulp and liquid to the vegetables in the sauté pan. Add the remaining ingredients except the olives and capers and cook for a further 2 minutes.

To remove the stones from the olives, roll them on a flat surface to loosen the stones and then remove them with a swivel vegetable peeler. Alternatively, use a cherry pitter. Slice the olives in quarters and add to the vegetables with the capers. Simmer, uncovered, over moderate heat for 15 minutes to evaporate most of the liquid. Adjust the seasoning and serve hot or cold.

The ruins of Selinunte on the coast of Sicily contain the remains of eight Doric temples dating from between 6 and 5 BC.

SERVES 6-8

Rice Salad Roman Style

Italians eat a great deal of rice and indeed it is a staple in the North almost to the same degree as pasta.

PREPARATION TIME: 10-15 minutes

COOKING TIME: 20-25 minutes

1 cup rice

⅔ cup uncooked cannellini beans

2 cloves garlic

½ tsp red pepper flakes

½ cup soft breadcrumbs soaked in

¼ cup beef broth and squeezed dry

½ cup oil

3 tbsps red wine vinegar

1 tsp salt

⅓ cup diced lean prosciutto crudo

4 slices slab bacon

1 can flat anchovy fillets, rinsed with cold water

8 large green olives

2 tbsps coarsely chopped fresh basil leaves

2 tbsps coarsely chopped fresh marjoram

Cook rice and beans separately in lightly salted water until tender. Drain and cool. Grind garlic and hot pepper in a mortar, add squeezed breadcrumbs and beat in oil, wine vinegar and salt. Put rice and beans in a salad bowl. Add prosciutto. Cut bacon into thin strips and saute in 1 tablespoon oil until crisp. Drain bacon and add to salad bowl. Stir in bread sauce. Roll anchovy fillets around olives and arrange them on top of salad as decoration. Sprinkle with basil and marjoram cut into rather large pieces. Chill. Serve either as a luncheon dish or as antipasto.

The colorful gardens of the Vestal Virgins in Rome.

SERVES 6
Pasta Salad

This popular Italian salad can be eaten as a main dish or as a side salad.

PREPARATION TIME: 15-20 minutes

4 cups cooked red kidney beans,
  drained
3 cups pasta shells or spirals,
  cooked
1 large green pepper, seeded and
  sliced into 1-inch long pieces
1 large red pepper, seeded and
  sliced into 1-inch long pieces
20-30 pitted black olives, sliced in
  half
1 tbsp capers
4-5 sprigs fresh parsley, chopped

DRESSING
1 cup olive oil
¼ cup lemon juice
2½ tsps finely chopped fresh basil
  leaves
1¼ tsps salt
½ tsp freshly ground black pepper
2 cloves garlic, peeled and minced
1 small head chicory

Combine the beans, pasta, peppers, olives, capers and parsley in a large bowl. Mix all the dressing ingredients together; add to the salad ingredients and toss together. Line the serving platter or bowl with chicory leaves; place the pasta salad in the center. Alternatively: add ½lb of thinly sliced salami or Italian sausages or canned sausages in brine cut into bite-size pieces.

Right: the bustling harbor at Camogli, in the Liguria region.

SERVES 4

Bean Salad

This quick bean salad is the ideal solution when the family needs an appetizing meal in a hurry.

PREPARATION TIME: 10 minutes
COOKING TIME: 15 minutes

3 cups macaroni
1 large can red kidney beans, drained
4 strips bacon, diced
1 onion, peeled and chopped
2 sticks celery, sliced diagonally

1-2 tbsps wine vinegar
3-4 tbsps olive oil
1 tsp chopped parsley
Salt
Pepper

Cook the macaroni in plenty of salted boiling water for 10 minutes, or until tender but still firm. Rinse in cold water and drain well. Heat a frying pan, and sauté bacon in its own fat until crisp. Add onion, and cook until soft. Mix vinegar, oil and parsley, and season well. Add bacon, onion, kidney beans and celery to macaroni. Pour over dressing and toss together.

A regatta on the Grand Canal in Venice brings out the
competitive spirit in the teams of gondoliers.

SERVES 4

Tomato Salad Rustica

An informal salad with a country flavor, this is perfect with barbecued meat, poultry or fish.

PREPARATION TIME: 20 minutes plus
30 minutes standing time

1lb tomatoes
1 onion
4-6 anchovies
Milk
2 tbsps capers

1 tsp chopped fresh oregano or
basil
6 tbsps olive oil
1 tbsp lemon juice

Soak the anchovies in a little milk before using, rinse, pat dry and chop. Cut the tomatoes into quarters and remove the cores. Slice each quarter in half again and place them in a serving bowl.

Slice the onion into rounds and then separate into rings. Scatter over the tomatoes. Cut the anchovies into small pieces and add to the tomatoes and onions along with the capers. Mix the herbs, salt, pepper, oil and lemon juice together until well emulsified and pour over the salad. Mix all the ingredients gently and leave to stand for about 30 minutes before serving.

Vietri Sul Mare on the rocky coastline of Salerno.

SERVES 4-6

Peas and Rice

"Risi e bisi" is a famous dish from the Veneto region of Italy. Serve as a side dish to roast dishes or pizzas.

PREPARATION TIME: 5 minutes
COOKING TIME: 25-30 minutes

⅓ cup bacon or prosciutto, as fat as possible
½ onion, chopped
¼ cup butter
1 tbsp olive oil
1lb fresh peas

Salt
1½ quarts chicken broth
1 cup rice
¼ cup shredded Parmesan cheese
6 sprigs parsley, chopped

Sauté chopped bacon and onion in half of the butter and oil. When onion is transparent, add peas; salt lightly, stir and add broth. Cover and cook over a moderate heat until the peas are half cooked. Add rice and stir with a wooden spoon, taking care not to crush the peas, and complete cooking. The rice will take about 17 minutes to cook. Before removing from the heat, stir in the remaining butter, Parmesan and parsley. Stir again, allow to stand for a few minutes and serve.

The dramatic contrast of ancient and modern in the Sicilian town of Agrigento.

SERVES 6-8

Sautéed Sliced Artichoke Bottoms with Parsley and Garlic

This unusual vegetable dish is perfect served with roast meat or as part of a large spread.

PREPARATION TIME: 10 minutes
COOKING TIME: 30-35 minutes

8 large artichokes
2 cloves garlic, chopped
7 tbsps olive oil

Salt and freshly ground pepper
6 sprigs parsley, chopped

Remove all the artichoke leaves and trim off choke, leaving only the fleshy bottom of the artichoke. Slice artichoke bottoms into strips. Sauté garlic in oil briefly, then add artichoke bottoms and season with salt and pepper. Cook for several minutes over high heat, then lower heat and continue cooking until artichokes are tender, about 30 minutes. Sprinkle finely chopped parsley over dish just before serving.

Above: the remains of the Roman Forum, whose breathtaking architecture once underlined Rome's status as the capital of the world.

SERVES 4

ennel au Gratin

verlooked for more common vegetables. Here it takes
tage, enhanced by a delicious cheese sauce.

PREPARATION TIME: 15 minutes
COOKING TIME: 25-30 minutes

ennel   ½ cup dry white wine
                                         4 tbsps cream
                                         ¾ cup shredded fontina cheese
Salt and freshly ground black
    pepper to taste   GARNISH
2 tbsps butter   1 tbsp chopped chives
1½ tbsps flour
½ cup milk

Trim both ends of the fennel – reserve any feathery tops for garnish. Peel off any
discolored patches from the fennel. Cut each head in half lengthwise. Put the fennel
into a pan of boiling water to which you have added the lemon juice and 1 tsp salt;
simmer steadily for 5 minutes. Drain the par-boiled fennel thoroughly. Melt the butter
in a pan and stir in the flour; gradually stir in the milk and white wine. Bring to the
boil and stir until lightly thickened. Beat in the cream, half the shredded cheese, and
salt and pepper to taste. Arrange the fennel in a lightly greased ovenproof dish and
spoon the sauce evenly over the top; sprinkle with the remaining shredded cheese.
Bake in the oven at 375°F for 25-30 minutes, until the sauce is golden. Garnish with
the chopped chives and any reserved pieces of feathery fennel.

*Above: sunset in Venice from the Rialto Bridge. Right: St Mark's
Square in Venice is a vast gathering place surrounded by many
beautiful buildings.*

MAKES 10

Chocolate Apricot Horns

This luxurious dessert is a wonderful treat which is both attractive and delicious.

PREPARATION TIME: 15 minutes
COOKING TIME: 15-20 minutes

8oz puff paste
Beaten egg to glaze
4oz semi-sweet chocolate
1 tbsp butter
2½ tbsps brandy

¾ cup apricot purée
¾ cup heavy cream, whipped

TO DECORATE
Chocolate curls

Roll out the paste into a rectangle about 10x13 inches and trim the edges. Cut into strips 1-inch wide. Dampen one long edge of each strip with water and wind round a metal cornet mold (start at the point and overlap the dampened edge as you go). Put the horns on a lightly dampened cookie sheet and chill for 15 minutes. Brush the horns with beaten egg and bake at 425°F for 15-20 minutes until golden brown. Leave for 5 minutes, before carefully removing the molds; cool the pastry horns on a wire rack. Melt the chocolate with the butter on a plate, over a pan of hot water; dip each of the horns into the chocolate. Mix the brandy with the apricot purée and spoon a little into each of the horns. Fit a fluted nozzle to a pastry bag and fill the pastry bag with the whipped cream. Push the cream into the horns. Decorate with chocolate curls.

Right: the Basilica of St Peter's in Rome, seen from the River Tiber.

Strawberries and Oranges

SERVES 4-6

This perfect summer dessert is simple to prepare and truly delicious.

PREPARATION TIME: 15 minutes plus chilling

2lbs strawberries
2 oranges

½ cup sugar cubes
¼ cup Liquore alla Mandarina

Hull and slice the strawberries; peel and slice the oranges. Mash half the strawberries with the sugar cubes and liqueur. Stir in the remaining fruit and chill for one hour. Serve in individual dishes.

SERVES 4

Fennel au Gratin

Fennel is often overlooked for more common vegetables. Here it takes centerstage, enhanced by a delicious cheese sauce.

PREPARATION TIME: 15 minutes
COOKING TIME: 25-30 minutes

4 medium-size heads of fennel
Juice of 1 lemon
Salt and freshly ground black
    pepper to taste
2 tbsps butter
1½ tbsps flour
½ cup milk

½ cup dry white wine
4 tbsps cream
¾ cup shredded fontina cheese

GARNISH
1 tbsp chopped chives

Trim both ends of the fennel – reserve any feathery tops for garnish. Peel off any discolored patches from the fennel. Cut each head in half lengthwise. Put the fennel into a pan of boiling water to which you have added the lemon juice and 1 tsp salt; simmer steadily for 5 minutes. Drain the par-boiled fennel thoroughly. Melt the butter in a pan and stir in the flour; gradually stir in the milk and white wine. Bring to the boil and stir until lightly thickened. Beat in the cream, half the shredded cheese, and salt and pepper to taste. Arrange the fennel in a lightly greased ovenproof dish and spoon the sauce evenly over the top; sprinkle with the remaining shredded cheese. Bake in the oven at 375°F for 25-30 minutes, until the sauce is golden. Garnish with the chopped chives and any reserved pieces of feathery fennel.

Above: sunset in Venice from the Rialto Bridge. Right: St Mark's Square in Venice is a vast gathering place surrounded by many beautiful buildings.

122

MAKES 10

Chocolate Apricot Horns

This luxurious dessert is a wonderful treat which is both attractive and delicious.

PREPARATION TIME: 15 minutes
COOKING TIME: 15-20 minutes

8oz puff paste
Beaten egg to glaze
4oz semi-sweet chocolate
1 tbsp butter
2½ tbsps brandy

¾ cup apricot purée
¾ cup heavy cream, whipped

TO DECORATE
Chocolate curls

Roll out the paste into a rectangle about 10x13 inches and trim the edges. Cut into strips 1-inch wide. Dampen one long edge of each strip with water and wind round a metal cornet mold (start at the point and overlap the dampened edge as you go). Put the horns on a lightly dampened cookie sheet and chill for 15 minutes. Brush the horns with beaten egg and bake at 425°F for 15-20 minutes until golden brown. Leave for 5 minutes, before carefully removing the molds; cool the pastry horns on a wire rack. Melt the chocolate with the butter on a plate, over a pan of hot water; dip each of the horns into the chocolate. Mix the brandy with the apricot purée and spoon a little into each of the horns. Fit a fluted nozzle to a pastry bag and fill the pastry bag with the whipped cream. Push the cream into the horns. Decorate with chocolate curls.

Right: the Basilica of St Peter's in Rome, seen from the River Tiber.

With its picturesque setting, the pretty town of Portofino, in Liguria, has become a popular retreat for holidaymakers.

SERVES 4

Vanilla Cream Melba

Do not be put off by the use of soup pasta, this quick and imaginative dessert tastes delicious.

PREPARATION TIME: 15 minutes
COOKING TIME: 10 minutes

⅔ cup soup pasta
1½ cups milk
2½ tbsps brown sugar
½ cup cream, lightly whipped
Few drops vanilla extract
1 can peach halves
1 tsp cinnamon

MELBA SAUCE
1 cup raspberries
2 tbsps powdered sugar

Cook pasta in milk and sugar until soft. Stir regularly, being careful not to allow it to boil over. Draw off heat and stir in vanilla extract. Pour pasta into a bowl to cool. When cool, fold in cream. Chill. Meanwhile, make melba sauce. Push raspberries through a strainer. Mix in powdered sugar to desired thickness and taste. Serve pasta with peach halves and melba sauce. Dust with cinnamon if desired.

The River Arno, spanned by the Ponte Vecchio – the oldest bridge in Florence.

SERVES 4-6

Profiteroles

Italians have an infamous love of sweet desserts. Profiteroles are certain to satisfy the most avid sweet tooth.

PREPARATION TIME: 1 hour 30 minutes

COOKING TIME: 30 minutes

PASTRY
⅓ cup butter
1 cup water
1 cup all-purpose flour
Pinch of salt
3 beaten eggs

FILLING
2 cups heavy cream
2 tbsps sifted powdered sugar
2 tbsps Liquore alla Mandarina

CARAMEL
1 cup sugar
½ cup water

Sift the flour and salt together. Melt the butter in a heavy saucepan with the water and bring to the boil. Remove from the heat. Add flour and salt mixture to the pan as soon as liquid has boiled. This should be carried out rapidly. Beat with a wooden spoon until glossy. This mixture should be the right consistency to form small balls at this stage. Turn out onto a plate and spread out to cool. Return it to the pan and gradually beat in the eggs. Fill a pastry bag with the paste. Attach a ¾-inch plain nozzle. Pipe the paste in small balls onto a greased cookie sheet. Make sure they are well apart. Bake in the oven at 325°F for 25 minutes until well risen and golden brown. They should be firm to the touch. Pierce each puff to allow the steam to escape, and return them to the oven for 2 minutes. Cool on a wire rack.

Filling
Whip the cream, fold in the sugar and the liqueur. Fill a pastry bag fitted with a plain nozzle with the cream and fill each of the cream puffs.

Caramel
Melt the sugar gently in a saucepan with the water and boil it until it turns brown and caramelizes. Cool until the caramel begins to thicken but not set and pour quickly, but gently, over the puffs. Leave to set and chill for ½ hour before serving.

Left: Venice's "streets" are her one hundred or so canals, some of which are no wider than five feet.

The coast at Amalfi is littered with numerous small coves and beaches.

SERVES 4

Cream Cheese Margherita

A delectable alternative to very sweet desserts; this unusual dish is subtle yet delicious.

PREPARATION TIME: 1 hour
COOKING TIME: 10 minutes

¾ cup soup pasta
½ cup light cream
8oz package cream cheese
½ tsp ground cinnamon
4 tbsps sugar
4 tbsps golden raisins

Juice and shredded rind of ½ a lemon

GARNISH
1 tbsp sliced almonds
Lemon peel, cut into slivers

Soak raisins in lemon juice for about 1 hour. Meanwhile, cook the pasta in plenty of boiling, lightly salted water until tender, stirring occasionally. Work the cream cheese, sugar and cream together until smooth. Beat in shredded lemon rind and cinnamon. Fold in pasta and raisins. Divide between individual dessert glasses or small dishes, and cover top with sliced almond and slivers of lemon peel. Chill before serving.

SERVES 6-8

Marsala Ice Cream Torte

Enjoying ice cream is a national pastime in Italy, and once you have sampled this special recipe you will understand why!

PREPARATION TIME: 30 minutes plus freezing time

COOKING TIME: 1 hour

Oil for greasing
2 cups sugar
3 egg whites
1 tbsp instant coffee

2 tbsps boiling water
1½ cups heavy cream
2 tbsps Marsala
½ pint chocolate ice cream

Lightly oil a cookie sheet and line the base of a 7-inch round, loose-bottomed cake pan with wax paper. Whisk the egg whites and gradually add the sugar and continue to whisk until stiff. Add the remaining sugar and whisk until it peaks. Fill a pastry bag fitted with a fluted nozzle with the meringue mixture. Pipe small rosettes onto the cookie sheet, keeping them well apart. Bake them in a preheated oven at 300°F for 1 hour; leave in the oven for a further 20 minutes, with the oven turned off. Remove the meringues from the oven and allow them to cool. Mix the coffee with the water in a small bowl. Whisk the cream until thick; fold in all but 4 of the meringues. Add the coffee and the Marsala, taking care not to crush the meringues. Fold in the ice cream. Use the mixture to fill the prepared cake pan. Cover and freeze until firm. Put the reserved meringues in the center of the torte. Remove from the freezer to the refrigrator ½ hour before serving.

Right: a fountain partially obscures the spectacular facade of St Peter's Church, Rome.

*The contrast between alpine meadows and high peaks make the
Dolomites a popular destination for walkers and climbers.*

SERVES 8

Chocolate Chip Ice Cream

Delight your family by treating them to this mouthwatering ice cream.

PREPARATION TIME: 30 minutes, plus freezing time
COOKING TIME: 6-8 minutes

¾ cup semi-sweet chocolate,
  chopped or shredded
1 cup milk
3 egg yolks

⅓ cup sugar
1 cup heavy cream, lightly
  whipped
½ cup finely chopped chololate

Stir the chopped or shredded chocolate into the milk in a small, heavy-based saucepan; stir over a gentle heat until the chocolate melts. Put the egg yolks into a bowl with the sugar and beat until thick and creamy. Add the chocolate milk and beat. Return the chocolate mixture to the saucepan and stir continuously over a moderate heat until the mixture is thick and will coat the back of a spoon. Strain the chocolate custard into a bowl and cool in the refrigerator. When quite cold, fold in the whipped cream. (If you are using a churn, pour in the mixture and follow the manufacturer's instructions, adding the chopped chocolate at the appropriate stage.) Pour into ice trays and freeze until the mixture begins to set around the edges. Pour into a bowl and beat. Stir in the chopped chocolate. Return the ice cream to the ice trays and freeze for 30 minutes. Repeat the beating and freezing method every 30 minutes, until the ice cream is thick. Freeze until firm.

The Cathedral and Leaning Tower of Pisa. The leaning tower was used by Galileo in his experiments on the law of gravity.

SERVES 4

Caramel Oranges

This classic Italian dessert looks wonderful and tastes delectable.

PREPARATION TIME: 25 minutes
COOKING TIME: 25 minutes in total

4 large oranges
1¼ cups sugar
1½ cups water

¼ cup extra water
2 tbsps brandy or orange liqueur

Use a swivel vegetable peeler to peel thin strips from two of the oranges. Take off any white pith and cut the strips into very thin julienne strips with a sharp knife. Place the julienne strips in a small saucepan, cover with water and bring to the boil.

Peel all the oranges with a serrated-edged knife. Cut the ends off first and then take the peel and pith off in very thin strips using a sawing motion. Cut the oranges horizontally into slices about ¼-inch thick. Drain the orange peel strips and leave to dry. Combine sugar and water in a heavy-based pan. Reserve ¼ cup water for later use. Place the mixture over medium heat until the sugar has dissolved. Add the drained orange peel strips to the pan. Boil the syrup gently, uncovered, for about 10 minutes or until the orange strips are glazed. Remove the strips from the pan and place on a lightly oiled plate. Return the pan to high heat and allow the syrup to boil, uncovered, until it turns a pale golden brown. Remove from the heat immediately and quickly add the extra water. Return to gentle heat and cook for a few minutes to dissolve hardened sugar. Remove the pan from the heat and allow to cool completely. Stir in the brandy.

Arrange the orange slices in a serving dish and pour over the cooled syrup. Pile the glazed orange strips on top and refrigerate for several hours, or overnight, before serving.

The Grand Canal is Venice's busiest waterway and a trip along it is the best way to view the city's splendid architecture.

SERVES 4

Almond Stuffed Figs

Surprise your guests with a dessert which is both healthful and delicious.

PREPARATION TIME: 25 minutes

4 large ripe figs
4 tbsps ground almonds
2 tbsps orange juice
2 tbsps finely chopped dried
   apricots

SAUCE
4 tbsps cream
Finely shredded rind of ½ orange

GARNISH
Wedges of ripe fig
Wedges of lime
Ground cinnamon

Make a cross cut in each fig, without cutting right down and through the base. Ease the four sections of each fig out, rather like a flower head. Mix the ground almonds with the orange juice and chopped dried apricots; press into the center of each fig. For the sauce: mix the cream with the orange rind, and thin down with a little water. Spoon a pool of orange flavored cream onto each of 4 small plates; sit a stuffed fig in the center of each one. Decorate with wedges of fig and lime and a sprinkling of ground cinnamon.

Above: the River Arno and the skyline of Florence from the Piazzale Michelangelo.

MAKES 10-12

Truffles

A great favorite with children and sweet-toothed adults. Serve with coffee as an after-dinner treat.

PREPARATION TIME: 15 minutes

1 cup semi-sweet chocolate,
    chopped or shredded
1 tbsp Marsala
2 tbsps unsalted butter
1 egg yolk

1 cup ground almonds
1 cup cake crumbs
¼ cup chocolate sprinkles

Melt the chocolate with the Marsala in a small bowl over a saucepan of hot water. Beat in the butter and egg yolk and remove the mixture from the heat. Stir in the ground almonds and cake crumbs to make a smooth paste. Divide into balls and roll them in the chocolate sprinkles until evenly coated.

The River Tiber in Rome is the third longest in Italy and is spanned by around twenty-five bridges.